Deep Learning and Artificial Intelligence

A Complete Guide to Building
Intelligent Apps for Beginners,
Applied Artificial Intelligence to Our
Future
(2 in 1 Book)

Book 1
Deep Learning

Concepts and Applications for
Beginners Guide to Building
Intelligent Systems

Book 2

Artificial Intelligence

How Artificial Intelligence Works
and How We Apply Artificial
Intelligence to Harness Its Power for
Our Future

MARK HOWARD

Table of Contents

CHAPTER 6: DEEP LEARNING APPLICATIONS
105

CHAPTER 5: NATURAL LANGUAGE PROCESSING 195

CHAPTER 6: RECOMMENDATION SYSTEM 215

CHAPTER 7: INTERNET OF THINGS 231

Text Copyright © Mark Howard

Legal & Disclaimer

The content and information contained in this book has been compiled from sources deemed reliable, and it is accurate to the best of the Author's knowledge, information and belief. However, the Author cannot guarantee its accuracy and validity and cannot be held liable for any errors and/or omissions. Further, changes are periodically made to this book as and when needed. Where appropriate and/or necessary, you must consult a professional (including but not limited to your doctor, attorney, financial advisor or such other professional advisor) before using any of the suggested remedies, techniques, or information in this book.

Upon using the contents and information contained in this book, you agree to hold harmless the Author from and against any damages, costs, and expenses, including any legal fees potentially resulting from the application of any of the information provided by this book. This disclaimer applies to any loss, damages or injury caused by the use and application, whether directly or indirectly, of any advice or information presented, whether for breach of contract, tort, negligence, personal injury, criminal intent, or under any other cause of action.

You agree to accept all risks of using the information presented inside this book.

You agree that by continuing to read this book, where appropriate and/or necessary, you shall consult a professional (including but not limited to your doctor, attorney, or financial advisor or such other advisor as needed) before using any of the suggested remedies, techniques, or information in this book.

Book 1

Deep Learning

Concepts and Applications for Beginners Guide to Building Intelligent Systems

Introduction

Congratulations on downloading *Deep Learning* and thank you for doing so.

Sometimes referred to as hierarchical learning or deep structured learning, deep learning is a single part of a broad family of machine learning methods. These methods are based on learning data representations instead of using task-specific algorithms. The learning could be unsupervised, supervised, or semi-supervised.

The architectures of deep learning like recurrent neural networks, deep belief networks, and deep neural networks have been used in fields such as board game programs, bioinformatics drug design, machine translation, social network filtering, audio recognition, natural language processing, speech recognition, and computer vision. In these applications, they have come up with results that can be compared to and has sometimes proven to be better than human experts.

These deep learning models are partially inspired by information processing, as well as the communication patterns within the human nervous system. There are various differences between the functional and structural properties when it comes to human brains, which means that they are incompatible with neuroscience evidence.

This book will give you the basics of deep learning to help get you started. Deep learning is only a small section of data science, but once you get the hang of it, everything else will fall into place.

There are plenty of books on this subject on the market, thanks again for choosing this one! Every effort was made to ensure it is full of as much useful information as possible, please enjoy!

Chapter 1: History

Rina Dechter introduced the machine learning community to deep learning in 1986. In the context of the Boolean threshold neurons, Igor Aizenbery introduced his colleagues to artificial neural networks in 2000.

In 1965, Lapa and Alexey Ivakhnenko published the first general multilayer, feed forward, deep, working algorithms for supervised perceptrons. A paper in 1971 described an eight-layer deep network that was trained using the group method of data handling algorithm.

Kunihiko Fukushima introduced the Neocognitron in 1980, which started other deep learning architectures, especially the ones created for computer vision. Yann LeCun and others used the "standard backpropagation algorithm" in 1989. This had been in use since the 1970s, but was referred to as the "reverse mode of automatic differentiation." He used the method on a deep neural network that was created for recognizing handwritten ZIP codes. The algorithm did work, but it had to be trained for three days.

Starting in 1991, these types of systems were used to find isolated 2D handwritten numbers, while also recognizing 3D objects by matching up 2D pictures with a 3D object model. One of the team members, Weng, suggested the brain doesn't follow a monolithic 3D object model, and that's when they published Cresceptron in 1992. This was a method that was used for performing 3D object recognition in scenes that were cluttered. Since the method used natural images, it began the general purpose of visual learning to find natural 3D worlds.

Cresceptron was created as a cascade of layers close in nature to Neocognitron. While the later needed human programmers to merge the features, the former learned an open amount of features in all layers without the need of supervision. Each of the features is represented using a convolution kernel. Cresceptron broke up all of the objects it had learned from a messy scene using what they called a back-analysis in the networks. Max pooling, which is now popular in deep neural networks, was first used by Cresceptron to lower the position resolution by using the cascade to make a better generalization.

Andre de Carvalho, as well as David Bisset and Mike Fairhurst, published their experimental results using a multi-layer Boolean neural network in 1994. This was also referred to as a weightless neural network, which was made up of a three-layer "self-organizing feature extraction neural network module" (SOFT). This was also followed by a "multi-layer classification neural network module" (GSN). These were both independently trained. All of the layers in the extraction module would extract the features with increasing complexity in regards to the last layer.

Brendan Frey, in 1995, showed that it was possible that a person could train a network that contained six layers that were connected and hundreds of hidden layers with an algorithm known as wake-sleep which was done in only two days. This was co-developed by Hinton and Peter Dayan. There are a lot of factors that can cause a speed to slow including the "vanishing gradient problem" which Sepp Hochreiter analyzed in 1991.

In the 2000s and 1990s, simpler models that had been created to use "task-specific handcrafted features," like support vector machines and Gabor filters were popular choices. This was due to ANNs' computational cost and a lower understanding of the way the brain wires up the biological networks.

For many years, deep and shallow learning of ANNs has been explored. None of these methods were able to outperform "non-uniform internal-handcrafting Gaussian mixture model/Hidden Markov model" (GMM-HMM) technology that was built on general speech models that had been discriminatively trained. Over the years, the main problems have been studied including a weak temporal correlation and gradient diminishing structure in the neural predictive models. Some of the other problems were the limited computing power and lack of training data.

The majority of researchers on speech recognition have changed their workings from neural networks to generative modeling. Exclusion would be the SRI International in the late '90s. The US government funded these with DARPA and NSA, and it looked at the deep neural networks in the speaker and speech recognition.

The team for speaker recognition was created by Heck found their first big success with these networks in processing speech in the "'98 National Institute of Standards and Technology speaker recognition evaluation." They may have found success with "deep neural networks for speaker recognition;" they were unable to demonstrate the same type of success when it to came to speech recognition.

The idea of bringing up "raw" features instead of optimization that was hand-crafted was first looked in as a successful architecture of "deep autoencoder" was used with linear filter-bank features on the "raw" spectrogram during the '90s. This showed superiority to the Mel-Cepstral features, which had been using a different "fixed transformation from spectrograms." The waveforms of speech later on created great large-scale results.

The majority of aspects around speech recognition were eventually controlled by a deep learning method known as "long short-term memory." This is a "recurrent neural network" that was released by Schmidhuber and Hochreiter in '97. The RNNs of LSTM found their way around the gradient problem and was able to learn "Very Deep Learning" tasks that would need a high amount of memories from several different events that had taken place over thousands of discrete times. This provided to be extremely important for speech.

By 2003, LSTM began to compete with what had been traditional recognizers. They later combined it with "connectionist temporal classification." In 2015, Google's speech recognition experienced a large leap of 49 percent with CTC-trained LSTM. This is what Google turned into their Google Voice Search.

A publication in 2006 showed the effectiveness of a "many-layered feed forward neural network" when it came to pre-training each individual layer and treating every layer in order as an "unsupervised restricted Boltzmann machine." This was made just a bit better through supervising backpropagation.

Deep learning is just a single area of amazing systems in several different disciplines, especially automatic speech recognition and computer vision. The results are normally used to evaluate sets like MNIST and TIMIT, and "large-vocabulary speech recognition tasks," which got better. The "convolutional neural networks" were replaced with ASR by CTC for LSTM, and they work a lot better than computer vision.

The idea of deep learning really started to impact things at the turn of the century, when CNNs were being used to process around ten to twenty percent of the checks that were written in the US. In 2010, industrial uses for this information started using "large-scale speech recognition."

The NIPS Workshop in 2009 found motivation through all of the limitations that came with "deep generative models of speech," as well as the chance that it gave for "capable hardware and large-scale datasets," which meant that DNNs could end up being practical. It was thought that the pre-trained DNNs made use of a "generative model of deep belief nets," and that this would help them fix the big problems that came along with the neural nets. Instead, they found out that they could replace the pre-training with a lot of data for the "straightforward backpropagation" when they used DNNs that was created with huge, content-dependent output layers and would end up creating error rates that were a lot lower than the GMM-HMM.

The main errors that these systems produced were very different. They offered a lot of technological insights into how they can use deep learning in their already well-working "speech decoding system" which was already being used with recognition systems.

Researchers in 2010 grew their deep learning from "TIMIT" to "large vocabulary recognition." They did this by creating larger output layers of a deep neural network built around the "context-dependent HMM states that were created using decision trees.

Chapter 2: Deep Learning

Over the past several years deep learning has worked its way into the language of business when conversations about artificial intelligence, analytics, and big data come up. And there is a good reason for that. Its approach to AI is showing a lot of promise when it comes to coming up with autonomous self-teaching systems. These things are revolutionizing a lot of industries.

Google uses deep learning for voice recognition algorithms. Amazon and Netflix use it to decide what it is that you are interested in watching or buying next. MIT researchers use it to predict the future. This very well established and still growing industry is always looking for a chance to sell these tools about how revolutionary it all is. But what is it exactly? Is this just some other fad that is used to push the old-fashioned AI on us by using some sexy new name?

It would probably be helpful to look at deep learning as the cutting-edge of the cutting-edge. Machine learning uses some of the main ideas of AI and focuses on figuring out some real-world problems using neural networks that are used to mimic a human brain's decision-making process. Deep learning likes to focus more on narrower subsets of machine learning tools and techniques, and then it will apply them to figure out almost any problem that needs thinking, whether artificial or human.

If you are just starting in the deep learning field, or if you have a bit of experience with neural networks a long time ago, you will probably find yourself a bit confused. A lot of people have been baffled by this, especially those who learned about neural networks in the 1990s and early 2000s.

How it Works

Basically, deep learning involves providing a computer system with a whole lot of data, which it will then use to make decisions about different types of data. The data will then be fed throughout a neural network, which is the same as machine learning. The networks are logical constructions which ask a bunch of binary true and false questions. They also extract a numerical value of the entire data collection which runs throughout them, and they classify them according to the answers that they get.

Since deep learning is mainly focused on coming up with these networks, they will then become what is known as a deep neural network. This is a logic network of complexity that is needed to handle the classifying data sets as large as Twitter's firehouse of tweets or Google's image library.

When you have data sets that are as comprehensive as these and logical networks that are created sophisticated enough to handle classification, it will end up being trivial for the computer to be able to take an image and tell you with a high probability of accuracy what a human would see it as.

Pictures is a perfect example of how all of this works because they typically have a lot of different elements, and they are easy for us to grasp the way a computer, which has a one-track calculation mind, can figure out how to interpret them just like we would. However, the great thing about deep learning is that it can be applied to all types of data, written words, speech, video, audio, and machine signals so that it can produce conclusions that appear to have come from a human, extremely fast humans. We're going to take a look at a practical example.

Take, for example, a system that was created to automatically record and report the number of vehicles of a certain make and model that travel across a public road. First, they would access a large database of the different car types which include their engine sound, shape, and size. This could be done in a manual fashion or, when it comes to advance use cases, it could be automatically compiled using a system if it has been programmed to scour the internet and take in all of the data that it discovers.

Then, it would have to take all of the data that it needs to process. This would be real-world data that contains the insights, which for this example would need to capture roadside cameras and microphones. By comparing the data from all of the sensors with the data that it has learned, it is then able to classify, with a probable accuracy, the passing vehicle and their make and model.

At this point, it is pretty much straightforward. The word deep comes in because the system, as time passes and it is able to gain more experience, is able to increase the probability that it will classify information correctly by training itself on all of the new data that it receives. Basically, it is able to learn from its own mistakes, just like humans. For example, it could end up incorrectly deciding that a certain vehicle is a certain type of make and model which was based upon their similar engine noise and size. It would overlook other differentiators that it thought would have a low probability of being important in making this particular decision. Since it has now learned that this differentiator is actually important in identifying two different vehicles, it will be able to improve the odds of it correctly picking the vehicle next time.

Chapter 3: Machine Learning

When you start talking about deep learning, the words data science, data analytics, and machine learning will come up a lot. In fact, we have already looked a little at machine learning. A lot of people will get these terms confused, and most aren't sure which one is which. In this chapter, we will look more at the differences between all of these things so that you have a clear understanding of what they all are.

Machine learning is the practice of using algorithms to learn from data and forecast possible trends. The traditional software is combined with predictive and statistical analysis to help find the patterns and get the hidden information that was based upon the perceived data. Facebook is a great example of machine learning implementation. Their machine learning algorithms collect information for each user. Based on a person's previous behavior, their algorithm will predict the interests of the person and recommend notifications and articles in their news feed.

Since data science is a broad term that covers several disciplines, machine learning works as a part of data science. There are various techniques used in machine learning such as supervised clustering and regression. But, the data that is used in data science may not have come from a machine or any type of a mechanical process. The biggest difference is that data science covers a broader spectrum and doesn't just focus on statistics and algorithms but will also look at the entire data processing system.

Data science can be viewed as an incorporation of several different parent disciplines including data engineering, software engineering, data analytics, machine learning, business analytics, predictive analytics, and more. It includes the transformation, ingestion, collection, and retrieval of large quantities of data, which is referred to as Big Data. Data science structures big data, finding the best patterns, and then advising business people to make the changes that would work best for their needs. Machine learning and data analytics are two tools of the many that data sciences use.

A data analyst is someone who is able to do basic descriptive statistics, communicate data, and visualize data. They need to have a decent understanding of statistics and a good understanding of databases. They need to be able to come up with new views and to perceive data as visualization. You could even go as far as to say that data analytics is the most basic level of data science.

Data science is a very broad term that encompasses data analytics and other several related disciplines. Data scientists are expected to predict what could happen in the future using past patterns. A data analyst has to extract the important insights from different sources of data. A data scientist will create questions and the data analyst will find the answers to them.

Machine learning, deep learning, data science, and data analytics are only a few of the fasted growing areas of employment in the world right now. Having the right combination of skills and experience could help you get a great career in this trending arena.

AI, Deep Learning, and Machine Learning

Artificial intelligence looks at how to create machines that are capable of fulfilling tasks that would normally require human intelligence. This loose definition basically tells you that AI encompasses several fields of research, from expert systems to genetic algorithms, and helps to provide a scope of arguments over what it means to be AI.

Machine learning has recently found a lot of success in the field of AI research. It has allowed computers to pass up or come very close to matching up human performances in all areas that range from face recognition to language and speech recognition.

Machine learning uses the process of teaching a computer system how to perform a certain task instead of programming it to perform certain tasks in a step-by-step manner.

Once training has been finished, the system is able to come up with accurate predictions when it receives certain data.

This all may sound dry, but the predictions could end up answering if a fruit in a picture is an apple or banana, if a person is walking in front of a self-driving vehicle, if the word written in a sentence means a hotel reservation or a paperback, if an email message is a spam, or recognizing speech well enough to create captions on videos on YouTube.

Normally, machine learning is broken into supervised learning, which is where the computer is taught things by example from data that has been labeled, and unsupervised learning, which is when the computer groups together similar information and find the anomalies.

Deep learning is a single area within the machine learning process whose capabilities are different from traditional shallow machine learning in many important areas. This allows computers to be able to figure a whole host of complex issues that wasn't able to be solved any other way.

A good example of a shallow machine learning task would be predicting that ice cream sales will be different depending on what the temperature is like outside. They make predictions with the use of only a couple of data features, and it is relatively straightforward. This can be carried out in a shallow technique, which is known as a linear regression with a gradient descent.

The problem comes in the fact that there are a large number of problems within the world that don't fit very well in such a simple model. One example of a complex real-world issue is being able to recognize handwritten numbers.

In order for this problem to be solved, the computer will have to cope with large variations in a way where data can be presented. Each digit that ranges from 0 to 9 can be written in a myriad of different ways. Even the size and shape of the handwritten digits are able to be written in several different ways depending on the person writing them and in certain circumstances.

Coping with all of the variables of these different features and the large mess of interactions between each of them is where deep neural networks and deep learning start to be useful. Neural networks, which we will cover more completely in a later chapter, are mathematical models whose structure is very loosely based on the brain.

Every neuron in the network is a function that will receive data through an input, it then transforms the data into a form that is more amenable, and it will then send it out through an output. These neurons can be viewed as layers.

Each of these networks has an input layer. This is where the starting data is fed in. They also have an output layer, which is what generates the last prediction. When it comes to a deep neural network, there are several hidden layers of neurons that are located between these output and input layers, and each one of them feeds data into the other. This is why you have the word deep in deep learning, as well as in deep neural networks. This references the number of hidden layers, which is normally more than three, located in the heart of these neural networks.

Neurons are believed to be activated once the sum of the values that are being inputted into the neuron has passed a certain threshold. The activation means is different depending on the layer it is in. In the first hidden layer, activation could mean that the image of the handwritten number may contain a certain combo of pixels that look like horizontal lines at the top part of the number seven. Like this, that first hidden layer would detect a lot of the important curves and lines that would eventually mix together to create the final number.

A real neural network would probably have several hidden layers and several neurons in every layer. All of the small curves and lines found on the first layer would be fed in the second hidden layer, and then detect how they are combined to create a recognizable shape that creates a certain digit, like the entire loop of the number six. Through this act of feeding data between the different layers, each layer will handle a higher-level of features.

How are these layers able to tell a computer the nature of a written number? All of the neuron layers provide a way for the network to create a rough hierarchy of different features that create the written number that is in question. For example, if the input shows an array of values that represent the separate pixels in the photo of a written number, the following layer could show a combination of these pixels into shapes and lines, the following layer would combine all of the shapes into specific images such as the loops in an eight or a triangle in four, and so on. When you slowly build up a picture of all of these features, a modern neural network is able to determine, with very good accuracy, the amount that is connected to the written number. In a similar manner, different types of these deep neural networks are able to be trained to pick up of faces in a picture or change audio into written words.

The process of creating these increasingly complex hierarchies of features of written digits out of nothing except pixels is taught through the network. The computer is able to learn because how the network can alter the importance of the connections between each layer's neurons. Each of the links has an attached value that is known as the weight which will end up modifying the value that is sent out by a neuron as it travels between each layer. By changing up the value of the different weight, and the value that is known as the bias, there is a possibility to emphasize or diminish how important the links are between the network and neurons.

For example, when it comes to recognizing a number that was handwritten, these different weights can be changed to show the importance of a certain pixel group that creates a line, or a pair of lines that intersect that create a number seven.

Chapter 4: Neural Networks

Neural networks, which are sometimes referred to as Artificial Neural Networks, are a simulation of machine learning and human brain functionality problems. You should understand that neural networks don't provide a solution for all of the problems that come up but instead provide the best results with several other techniques for various machine learning tasks. The most common neural networks are classification and clustering, which could also be used for regression, but you can use better methods for that.

A neuron is a building unit for a neural network, which works like a human neuron. A typical neural network will use a sigmoid function.

This is typically used because of the nature of being able to write out the derivative using f(x), which works great for minimizing error.

Even though it has found new fame, the idea of these neural networks isn't actually new. In 1958, the psychologist, Frank Rosenblatt, tried to create "a machine which senses, recognizes, remembers, and responds like the human mind" and he named his creation Perceptron. He didn't come up with this out of thin air. Actually, his work was inspired by the works of Walter Pitts and Warren McCulloch from the 1940s.

Let's look at what a Perceptron is. Dendrites are extensions that come off the nerve cell. These are what get the signals, and they then send them onto the cell body, which processes the stimulus and then will make a decision to either trigger a signal or not. When a cell chooses to trigger a signal, the cell body extension known as an axon will trigger a chemical transmission at its end to a different cell. There is no need to feel like you have to memorize any of this. We aren't actually studying neuroscience, so you only need a vague impression of how this works.

Perceptron looks similar to an actual neuron because they were inspired by the way actual neurons work. Keep in mind; it was only inspired by a neuron and in no way acts exactly like a real one. The way a Perceptron processes data is as such:

1. There are small circles on the left side of the Perceptron which are the "neurons" and they have x subscripts 1, 2,..., m that carries data input.

2. All of the inputs are multiplied by a weight, which is labeled using a

subscript 1, 2, ... , m, along with a long arrow called the synapse and travels to the big circle in the middle. So you will have w1 * x1, w2 * x2, w3 * x3, and so on.

3. After all of the inputs have been multiplied by the weight, you will sum them all up and add a bias that had been pre-determined.

4. The results are then pushed onto the right. You will then use the step function. All of these tells that if the number you get from step three is greater than or equal to zero, you will receive a one as your output, otherwise, if your result is lower than zero, the output will be zero.

5. You will get an output of either zero or one.

If you were to switch the bias and place it on the right in the activation function such as "*sum(wx)* ≥ *-b*" the –b would be known as a threshold value. With this, if the sum is higher than or equal to your threshold, then your activation trigger is one. Otherwise, it would come out to be zero. Pick the one that helps you understand this process because both of these representations are interchangeable.

Now, you have a pretty good understanding of how a Perceptron works. All it's made up of is some mechanical multiplications, which then make summations, and then ultimately give you activation, and that will give you an output.

Just to make sure that you fully understand this, let's have a look at a really simple example that is not really realistic. Let's assume that you have found extreme motivation after you have read this book and you have to decide if you are going to study deep learning or not. You have three major factors that will help you make your decision:

1. Will you be able to make more money once you master deep learning: 0 – No, 1 – Yes.

2. Is the needed programming and mathematics simple: 0 – No, 1 – Yes.

3. You are able to use deep learning immediately and not have to get an expensive GPU: 0 – No, 1 – Yes.

Our input variables will be x1, x2, and x3 for all of the factors, and we'll give them each a binary value since they are all simple yes or no questions. Let's assume that you really love deep learning and you are now ready to work through your lifelong fear of programming and math. You also have some money put away to invest in the expensive Nvidia GPU that will train the deep learning model. You can assume that both of these have the same importance because both of them can be compromised. But, you really want to be able to make extra money once you have spent all of the energy and time into learning about deep learning. Since you have a higher expectation of ROI, if you can't make more moolah, you aren't going to waste your time on learning deep learning.

Now that you have a decent understanding of the decision preferences, we can assume that you have a 100 percent probability of making extra cash once you have learned deep learning because there's plenty of demand for a less supply. That means $x1 = 1$. Let's assume that programming and math are extremely hard. That means $x2 = 0$. Finally, let's assume that you are going to need a powerful GPU such as a Titan X. That means $x3 = 0$. Okay, now that you have the inputs, you can initialize your weights. We're going to try $w1 = 8$, $w2 = 3$, $w3 = 3$. The higher the value for the weight, the bigger influence it has with the input. Since the money you will make is more important, your decision for learning deep learning is, $w1$ is greater than $w2$, and $w1$ is greater than $w3$.

Let's say that the value of the threshold is five, which equals the bias of negative five. We add everything together and add in the bias term. Since the threshold value is five, you will decide to learn deep learning if you are going to make more money. Even if the math turns out to be easy and you aren't going to have to buy a GPU, you won't study deep learning unless you are able to make extra money later on.

Now, you have a decent understanding of bias and threshold. With a threshold as high as five, that means the main factor has to be satisfied in order for you to receive an output of one. Otherwise, you will receive a zero.

The fun part comes next: varying the threshold, bias, and weights will provide you with different possible decision-making models. With our example, if you lower your threshold from five to three, then you will get different scenarios where the output would be one.

Despite how well loved these Perceptrons were, the popularity faded quietly due to its limitations. Later on, people realized that multi-layer Perceptrons were able to learn the logic of an XOR gate, but this requires the use of back propagation so that the network can learn from its own problems. Every single deep learning neural networks are data-driven. If you are looking at a model and the output it has is different from the desired output, you will have to have a way to back propagate the error information throughout the network in order to let the weight know they need to adjust and fix themselves by a certain amounts. This is so that, the real outputs from the model will start getting closer in a gradual way to the desired output with each round of testing.

As it turned out when it comes to the more complicated tasks that involved outputs that couldn't be shown with a linear combination of inputs, meaning the outputs aren't linearly separable or non-linear, the step function will not work because the back propagation won't be supported. This requires that your activation function should have meaningful derivatives.

Here's just a bit of calculus: a step function works as a linear activation function where your derivative comes out to 0 for each of the inputs except for the actual point of 0. At the point of 0, your derivative is going to be undefined because the function becomes discontinuous at this point. Even though this may be an easy and simple activation function, it's not able to handle the more complicated tasks.

Sigmoid function: $f(x) = 1/1+e^{-x}$

Perceptrons aren't stable when it comes to being a neural network relationship candidate. Look at it like this: this person has major bipolar issues. There comes a day (if $z < 0$), they are all "down" and "quiet" and doesn't give any response. The next day (if $z \geq 0$), they are all of a sudden "lively" and "talkative" and is talking nonstop. A huge change, isn't it? Their mood doesn't have any transition, and you're not sure if it is going to go up or down. This is a step function.

Just a bit of a switch in each of the weights within the input of the network may cause a neuron to flip from zero to one, which could end up affecting the behavior of the hidden layer, and this would cause a problem for the outcome. It's important that you have a learning algorithm that improves the network because it slows the change of weights without any sudden jumps. If you aren't able to use step functions to slowly change up the weight values, then you shouldn't use it.

We are now going to say goodbye to the Perceptron with a step function. A new partner to use in your neural network is the sigmoid neuron. This is done by using the sigmoid function, which is written above. The only thing that is going to change is the activation function, and all the other stuff that you have learned up to this point about a neural network is going to work the same for the new neuron type.

If the function looks strange or a little abstract, you don't need to focus a lot on the details such as the Euler's number 'e' or the way a person was able to create such a crazy function. For the people that aren't all that math savvy, the only thing that you really need to worry about is that you need to know the curve, and then its derivative.

1. A sigmoid function will produce results close to a step function in that the results will be either zero or one. The curve will cross at the 0.5 point at z=0, which you are then able to set function rules. This could be if the neuron's output is more or the same as 0.5, the output would be zero, and if the output ends up being less than 0.5, the output would be zero.

2. A sigmoid function's curve won't have a jerk. The curve will be smooth with a simple derivative of σ(z) * (1-σ(z)). This is differentiable in all areas of the curve.

3. If z ends up being negative, the output is going to be around zero. If z ends up being positive, the output will end up being around one. But when z=0 and z aren't too large or too small, you will get a relatively more deviation as the z changes.

A sigmoid function will introduce you to a non-linearity that will be added to the neural network. Non-linear only means that the output that you end up receiving isn't going to be able to be shown as a linear combination.

These non-linear functions will give you a new representation of your original data, and it will end up allowing for non-linear boundaries, like XOR. When you have XOR, if two of these neurons were placed in your hidden layers, you could change your original 2D figure to a 3D figure in a different area.

When it comes to linearity and non-linearity, things can become quite confusing. That's why, if you are serious about learning deep learning, it's important that you do plenty of studying on these subjects. Hopefully, though, you have a bit of a sense as to the reason why non-linear activation functions are important, but if you don't quite understand, it's okay. Allow yourself some time to take all of the information.

For a neural network to learn, you have to adjust the weights to get rid of most of the errors, as you have learned. This can be done by performing back propagation of the error. When it comes to a simple neuron that uses the

Sigmoid function as its activation function, you can demonstrate the error as we did below. We can consider that in a general case, the weight is termed as W and the inputs as X.

With this equation, the weight adjustment can be generalized, and you would have seen that this will only require the information from the other neuron levels. This is why this is a robust mechanism for learning, and it is known as the back propagation algorithm.

To practice this, we can write out a simple JavaScript application that uses two images and will apply a filter to a specific image. All you will need is an image you want to change and fill in its filename where it says to in the code.

```
" import Jimp = require("jimp");
Import Promise from "ts-promist";
Const synaptic = require("synaptic");
Const _ = require("lodash");
```

```
Const Neuron = synaptic.Neuron,
    Layer = synaptic.Layer,
   Network = synaptic.Network,
  Trainer = synaptic.Trainer,
  Architect = synaptic.Architect;
Function getImgData(filename) {
  Return new Promise((resolve, reject) => {
      Jimp.read(filename).then((image) => {
        Let inputSet: any = [];
        Image.scan(0, 0, image.bitmap.width,
image.bitmap.height, function (x, y, idx) {
            Var red = image.bitmap.data[idx
+ 0];
            Var          green          =
image.bitmap.data[idx + 1];

            inputSet.push([re, green]);
        });
      Resolve(inputSet);
    }).catch(function (err) {
      Resolve([]);
```

```
        });
    });
}
Const      myPerceptron      =      new
Archietect.Perceptron(4, 5);
Const trainer = new Trainer(myPerceptron);
Const traininSet: any = [];
getImgData('            imagefilename.jpg').
then((inputs: any) => {

getImageData('imagefilename.jpg').then((outpu
ts: any) => {
        for (let i=0; I < inputs.length; i++) {
            trainingSet.push({
                input: _.map(inputs[i], (val: any)
=> val/255),
                output: _.map(outputs[i], (val:
any) => val/255)
            });
        }
        Trainer.train(trainingSet, {
```

```
Rate:.1,
Interations: 200,
Error: .005,
Shuffle: true,
Log: 10,
Cost: Trainer.cost.CROSS_ENTROPY
});
Jimp.read('yours.jpg').then((image) =>
{
    Image.scan(0, 0, image.bitmap.width,
image.bitmap.height, (x, y, idx) => {
        Var red = image.bitmap.data[idx
+ 0];
        Var green = image.bitmap.data
[idx + 1];
        Var out –
myPerceptron.activate([red/255, green/255);
        Image.bitmap.data[idx + 0] =
_.round(out[0] * 255);
        Image.bitmap.data[idx + 1] =
_.round(out[1] * 255);
```

```
});

Console.log('out.jpg');

Image.write('out.jpg');

}).catch(function (err) {

Console.error(err);

});

});

}); "
```

Chapter 5: Algebra

Linear algebra is a mathematics branch that handles vector spaces. It underpins a huge amount of data science techniques and concepts, which means that it is important to learn as much as possible.

Vectors

Vectors are objects that you can add together to make new vectors, and they can be multiplied by scalars to make new vectors as well. Vectors are points located in a finite space. While you may not view your data as a vector, they are great ways to represent numeric information.

If you are dealing with ages, heights, and weights of a large group of people, you could treat this data like three-dimensional vectors: age, weight, height. If you are teaching a class that has four exams throughout the semester, you could treat these grades as a four-dimensional vector: test1, test2, test3, test4.

One of the easiest from-scratch approaches is to show your vectors as a number list. This list of three numbers will correspond to a single vector in your three-dimensional space, and so on:

" height_weight_age = [70,

170,

40]

Grades = [95,

80,

75,

62] "

A problem that comes with this approach is that you are going to want to perform some arithmetic on all of the vectors. Since Python lists don't work as vectors, and as such don't give you any tools for vector arithmetic, you will have to create these types of tools yourself. Let's see how that would work.

To start out, you will have to have two vectors. Vectors will add component-wise. All this means is that when you have two vectors, a and b, and they have the same length, they have a sum that has a first element of a[0] + b[0], and a second element of a[1] + b[1], and so on. If they don't have the same length, then they can't be added in.

If you were to add in the vectors [2, 3] and [3, 2], then you would get [2 + 3, 3 + 2] or [5, 5].

This can easily be used by zipping all of the vectors together and then making use of a comprehension to add in all of the corresponding elements.

" def vector_add(a, b):

Return [a_i + b_i

For a_i, b_i in zip (a, b)] "

In a similar manner, you can subtract your two vectors by getting rid of the corresponding elements.

" def vector_substract(a, b):

Return [a_i – b_i

For a_i, b_i in zip (a, b)] "

There may be times when you need to sum a vector list. This means that you will want to make a new vector which is the sum of the entire first elements, and the second vector should be the sum of the second elements, etc.

The easiest way to do this is to take it one vector at a time.

" def vector_sum (vectors) :

Result = vectors[0]

For vector in vectors [1:] :

Result = vector_add(result, vector)

Return result "

When you really think about what we are doing, we are only reducing the vector list with vector_add. This means that we are able to rewrite this using higher-order function, such as:

" def vector_sum(vectors) :

Return reduce(vector_add, vectors) "

Or you could:

" Vector_sum = partial(reduce, vector_add) "

Next, you will find that you have to multiply your vector by a scalar. You can do this by multiplying every vector element by this number.

" def scarlar_multiply (c, a):

*Return [c * a_i for a_i in a] "*

This is going to give you the ability to compute the component-wise means of your same-sized vector lists.

" def vector_mean(vectors):

N = len(vectors)

Return scalar_multiply(1/n, vector_sum (vectors)) "

One of the lesser known tools is the dot product. This product is created through the sum of two vectors and their component-wise products.

" def dot(a, b):

*Return sum(a_i * b_i*

For a_i, b_i in zip(a, b)) "

This product will measure how far *vector a* will extend in *vector b*'s direction. One example would be if b = [1, 0], then dot (a, b) is only the first element of a. A different way to do this is by saying it is the length of the vector you would see if you were to project *point a* to *point b*.

When you use this, it becomes simple to discover the sum of the vector's squares.

" def sum_of_squares (a):

Return dot (a, a) "

And this can then be used to figure out the length or magnitude.

" import math

Def magnitude(a):

Return math.sqrt(sum_of_square(a)) "

At this point, you now have the pieces you need to figure out the space between your two vectors, as you can see in this equation:

$$\sqrt{(a_1 - b_1)^2 + ... + (a_n - b_n)^2}$$

" *def squared_distance(a, b) :*

    Return sum_of_squares(vector_subtract (a, b))

Def distanc(a, b) :

    Return mathsqrt(squared_distance(a, b))

"

You can write the equivalent to get a clearer image of what we're looking at.

" *def distanc(a, b) :*

    Return magnitude(vector_substract (a, b)) "

This is a pretty good amount of information to help you get started with vectors. It's important that you take the time to study them even further if you are still unsure of how it works.

Note: When it comes to vector lists, it works well for exposition, but it doesn't do much for performance. The NumPy library should be where you turn for production code. This library has the high-performance array classes that you will need, and it has arithmetic operations.

Matrices

These are two-dimensional number sets. The matrices will be represented as lists of lists. Each of the inner lists will have the same size and will represent a matrices row. If K is a matrix, then K[c] [d] would be the d column and c row elements. Mathematical convention dictates that matrices are represented by capital letters. You can see this here:

" K = [[1, 2, 3],

[4, 5, 6]]

L = [[1, 2],

[3, 4],

[5, 6]] "

Note: When it comes to mathematics, the first row of a matrix would be labeled "row 1" and the first column would be named "column 1." Since this is using a Python list, which gets indexed at zero, our first matrix row will be labeled "row 0" and the first column will be labeled "column 0."

Since we are using list-of-lists representation, our matrix K will have "len(K) rows and len(K[0]) columns." You can look at the shape.

" def shap(K) ;

Num_rows = len(K)

Num_cols = len(K[0]) if K else 0

Return num_rows, num_cols "

When you have a matrix with d columns and c rows, it is called c X d matrix. You are able to view the rows of a c X d matrix as length c's vector, and every column is the vector length d.

" def get_row(K, c) :

Return K[c]

Def get_column (K, d):

Return [K_c [d]

For K_c in K] "

You will also want to make a matrix based on the shape and a function to create the elements. This can be done through a nested list of comprehension.

" def make_matrix(num_rows, num_cols, entry_fn) :

Return [[entry_fn (c, d)

For d in range (num_cols)]

For c in range (num_rows)] "

By using this function, you can create a five-by-five identity matrix that has a 1s on the diagonal and elsewhere would be a 0s.

" def is_diagonal (c, d) :

    Return 1 if c == d else 0

Identity_matrix = make_matrix (5, 5, is_diagonal)

These matrices end up being important for many different reasons.

A matrix can be used to represent a set of data that consists of several vectors by simply looking at each of the vectors as a row for your matrix. An example would be if you have the ages, heights, and weights for 1,000 people, you are able to place them in a 1,000 X 3 matrix.

" data = [[70, 170, 40],

    [65, 120, 26],

    [77, 250, 19],

    # ...

] "

You are also able to use c X d matrix to show a linear function that will map your c-dimensional vectors to your d-dimensional vectors. There are a lot of concepts and techniques that will involve these types of functions.

The third thing you can do with matrices is to use them to represent binary relationships. One representation of an edge of a network is to show them as a collection pair (c, d). But another way you could do this is to make matrix K like K[c] [d] so one of the nodes c and d are connected, and if not, they are zero.

In the former representation you would have:
" relationships = [(0, 1), (0, 2), (1, 2), (1, 3), (2, 3), (3, 4),

(4, 5), (5, 6), (5, 7), (6, 8), (7, 8), (8, 9)] "

This could also be shown as:

" relationships = [[0, 1, 1, 0, 0, 0, 0, 0, 0, 0],

[1, 0, 1, 1, 0, 0, 0, 0, 0, 0],

[1, 1, 0, 1, 0, 0, 0, 0, 0, 0],

[0, 1, 1, 0, 1, 0, 0, 0, 0, 0],

[0, 0, 0, 0, 1, 0, 1, 1, 0, 0],

[0, 0, 0, 0, 0, 1, 0, 0, 1, 0],

[0, 0, 0, 0, 0, 1, 0, 0, 1, 0],

[0, 0, 0, 0, 0, 0, 1, 1, 0, 1],

[0, 0, 0, 0, 0, 0, 0, 0, 1, 0]] "

If you don't have many connections, then this wouldn't be a very efficient representation because you will more than likely have a lot of stored zeros. However, when you use a matrix representation, it will be a lot faster to check if the nodes connect. When doing this, you will only need to do this for a single matrix lookup instead of inspecting each edge.

" relationships [0] [2] == 1

relationships [0] [8] == 1 "

If you are looking to figure a nodes connection, you are going to have to look at each row or column that corresponds with the node.

"friends_of_five = [c

For c, is_friend in enumerate(relationships[5])

If is_friend] "

In the past, you may have added a connections list to all of the node objects to speed up the process, but when it comes to evolving a large graph that would end up being a bit too expensive, it would be hard to maintain.

Discrete Versus Continuous

We are going to be looking at discrete variables. Discrete variables are variables that come from a limited set. They can also include numbers with decimals depending on your variable set, but this rule has to be established. For example, if you have the number 3.578 representing the number of medical procedures that a person has had in their life, that's not possible. Even if this was just the average, it is still misleading.

You can't come out with the odds that a person has had 3.578 medical procedures in their life. They would have either had three or four. If you were looking at procedures, you would see numbers like this:

- Numbers of procedures

    o 1

    o 2

    o 3

- Odds of having that number of procedures in a year

  - 25%

  - 25%

  - 50%

When you look at continuous variables, they can't be visualized in a table. Instead, these variables have to be given in a formula as there is an infinite number of variables. An example of an input variable could be 2, 2.9, 2.99, 2.999, 2.9999 … n.

Examples of these variables could be age, weight, and so one. A person isn't just 32. They are typically 32 years old, 195 days, 2 hours, 1 second, 4 milliseconds. Technically, these variables could represent any single moment in time, and every interval contains infinite intervals.

Poisson Distribution

$$p(x; \lambda) = \frac{e^{-\lambda} \lambda^x}{x!} \; for \; x = 0, 1, 2, ...$$

A Poisson distribution equation is used to figure out how many events could happen during a continuous interval of time. One example would be the number of phone calls that could happen during a certain time or the number of people that could end up in a queue.

This is actually a fairly simple equation to remember. The symbol is known as a lambda. This is what represents the average amount of events that happen during a certain interval of time.

An example of this distribution equation is to figure out the loss in manufacturing sheets of metal with a machine that has X flaws that happen per yard. Let's say that the error rate is two errors per yard of metal. Now, figure out what the odds are that the two errors would occur in a single yard.

Binomial Distribution

This is one of the most common and the first taught distribution in a basic statistics class. Let's say our experiment is flipping a coin. Specifically, the coin is flipped only three times. What are the odds that the coin will land on heads?

Using combinatorics, we know that there are 2^3 or eight different results combinations. By graphing the odds of getting 3 heads, 2 heads, 1 heads, and 0 heads. This is your binomial distribution. On a graph, this will look just like a normal distribution. This is because binomial and normal distributions are very similar. The difference is that one is discrete and the other is continuous.

Probability Density Function

If you have ever taken a basic statistics class, you know this function better than you think. Do you remember standard deviations? How about when you calculated the odds between the standard and average deviation? Did you realize that you were using a calculus concept known as integrals? Now, think about the space under the curve.

With this, we can assume that the space under the curve could be from negative infinity to positive infinity, or it could be a number set like the sides of a die.

But the value under the curve is one, so you would be calculating the space fewer than two points in the curve. If we go back to the sheet metal example, trying to find the odds that the two errors occur is a bit of a trick question. These are discrete variables and not continuous.

A continuous value would be zero percent.

Since the value is discrete, the integer will be whole. There wouldn't be any values between one and two, or between two and three. Instead, you would have 27% for two. If you wanted to know a value between two and three, what would the answer be?

PDF and the cumulative distribution function are able to take on continuous and discrete forms. Either way, you want to figure out how dense the odds are that fall under a range of points or a discrete point.

Cumulative Distribution Function

This function is the integral of the PDF. Both of these functions are used to provide random variables. To find the odds that a random variable is lower than a specific value, you would use the cumulative distribution function.

The graph shows the cumulative probability. If you were looking at discrete variables, like the numbers on a die, you would receive a staircase looking graph. Every step up would have 1/6 of the value and the previous numbers.

Once you reach the sixth step, you would have 100%. This means that each one of the discrete variables has a 1/6 chance of landing face up, and once it gets to the end, the total is 100%.

ROC Curve Analysis

Data science and statistics both need the ROC analysis curve. It shows the performance of a model or test by looking at the total sensitivity versus its fall-out rate.

This plays a crucial role when it comes to figuring out a model's viability. However, like a lot of technological leaps, this was created because of war. During WWII, they used it to detect enemy aircraft. After that, it moved into several other fields. It has been used to detect the similarities of bird songs, the accuracy of tests, the response of neurons, and more.

When a machine learning model is run, you will receive inaccurate predictions. Some of the inaccuracy is due to the fact that it needed to be labeled, say true, but was labeled false. And others need to be false and not true.

What are the odds that the prediction is going to be correct? Since statistics and predictions are just supported guesses, it becomes very important that you are right. With a ROC curve, you are able to see how right the predictions are and using the two parables, figure out where to place the threshold.

The threshold is where you choose if the binary classification is false or true, negative or positive. It will also make what your Y and X variables are. As your parables reach each the other, your curve will end up losing the space beneath it. This shows you that the model is less accurate no matter where your threshold is placed. When it comes to modeling most algorithms, the ROC curve is the first test performed. It will detect problems very early by letting you know if your model is accurate.

Bayes Theorem

This is one of the more popular ones that most computer-minded people need to understand. You can find it being discussed in lots of books. The best thing about the Bayes theorem is that it simplifies complex concepts. It provides a lot of information about statistics on just a few variables.

It works well with conditional probability, which means that if this happens, it will play a role in the resulting action. It will allow you to predict the odds of your hypothesis when you give it certain points of data.

You can use Bayes to look at the odds of somebody having cancer, based upon age, or if spam emails are based on the wording of the message.

The theorem helps lower your uncertainty. This was used in WWII to figure out the locations of U-boats and predict how the Enigma machine was created to translate codes in German.

K-Nearest Neighbor Algorithm

This is one of the easiest algorithms to learn and use, so much so that Wikipedia refers to it as the "lazy algorithm."

The concept of the algorithm is fewer statistics based and more reasonable deduction. Basically, it tries to identify the groups that are closest to each other. When k-NN is used on a two-dimensional model, it will rely on Euclidian distance.

This only happens if you are working with a one norm distance as it relates to square streets, and those cars can travel in a single direction at a time. The point I'm making is that the models and objects in this rely on two dimensions, just like the classic xy graph.

k-NN tries to identify groups that are situated around a certain number of points. K is the specified number of points. There are certain ways to figure out how big your k needs to be because it is an inputted variable that the data science system or user has to pick.

This model is perfect for feature clustering, basic market segmentation, and finding groups that are among specific data points. The majority of programming languages will let you implement in a couple of code lines.

Bagging or Bootstrap Aggregating

Bagging will involve making several models of one algorithm like a decision tree. Each one of them will be trained on the different bootstrap sample. Since this bootstrapping will involve sampling with replacement, some of your data won't be used in all of the trees.

The decisions trees that are made are created with different samples, which will help to solve the problem of sample size overfitting. Decision trees that are created in this way will help lower the total error since the variance will continue to lower with every tree that is added, without increasing the bias.

A random forest is a bag of decision trees that use subspace sampling. There is only one selection of the trees features that are considered at the split of each node, which removes the correlation of the trees in your forest.

These random forests also have their own built-in validation tool. Since there is only a percentage of this data that gets used for every model, the error of the performance can be figured out using only 37% of the sample that was left by the models.

This was only a basic rundown of some statistical properties that are helpful in data science. While some data science teams will only run algorithms in R and Python libraries, it's still important to understand these small areas of data science. They will make easier abstraction and manipulation easier.

Chapter 6: Deep Learning Applications

As you have learned so far, deep learning is changing how everybody looks at technology. A lot of excitement swirls around artificial intelligence as well as its branches of deep learning and machine learning. With the huge computational power that machines have, they are now able to translate speech and recognize objects in real time. Finally, artificial intelligence is getting smart.

It is believed that there are many deep learning applications that will affect your life in the very near future. In fact, they are probably already making a huge impact. In just the next five to ten years, deep learning development languages, tools, and libraries will end up being the standard components of all software development toolkits.

Let's look at some of the top deep learning applications that will end up ruling our world in 2018 and beyond.

Self-Driving Cars

Companies that work to build driver assistance services for cars, and full-blown self-driving cars just like Google's, have to teach the computer system how to use all, or at least, the key parts of driving by using digital sensor system instead of needing a human's sense. In order to do this, companies will have to start by training algorithms to use a lot of data. This can be looked at as a child learning through replication and experiences. All of these services could end up providing some unexpected business models for several companies.

Healthcare

Skin or breast cancer diagonostics? Monitoring and mobile apps? Maybe a personalized and predictive medicine on the basis of Biobank data? Artificial intelligence is reshaping healthcare, life sciences, and medicine as an industry. AI type innovations are advancing the future of population health and precision medicine management in ways that nobody would have ever believed. Computer-aided diagnosis, decision support tools, quantitative imaging, and computer-aided detection will all play very large roles in the future.

Voice-Activated Assistants and Voice Search

This is probably one the most popular uses for deep learning. All of the big tech giants have made large investments in this area. You can find voice-activated assistants on almost every smartphone. Siri has been available for use since October 2011. The assistant for Android, Google Now, was launched just a year after Siri. Microsoft has introduced the newest assistant in the form of Cortana.

Automatically Placing Audio in Silent Movies

When it comes to this, the system synthesizes the sounds that are similar to the silent movies. This system was trained with a thousand examples from different videos with sounds of a drumstick hitting different types of surfaces and coming up with different types of sounds. Deep learning models associate the frames of the video with a pre-recorded sound database so that it can choose a sound to play and matches up the best with the things going on in the scene.

They use a Turing Test to evaluate the system such as a setup where humans will have to figure out if the video has real or fake sounds. This uses applications of LSTM as well as RNN.

Automatic Machine Translation

This process is where a given word, sentence, or phrase is said in one language and then automatically translated to another language. This technology has been around for a while, but deep learning has gotten the best results in two areas:

Image translations

Text translations

These text translations can be done without the need for pre-processing the sequence, which allows the algorithm to be able to learn the dependencies between the word and the new language mapping.

Automatic Text Generation

This task is one of the most interesting. This is where a body of text has been learned, and new text is created either character-by-character or word-by-word. This model can learn how to capture text styles, forms of sentences, punctuations, and spelling in the body. Large recurrent neural networks are helpful when it comes to learning the relationship between different items in an input string sequence, and it will then generate text.

If you want to learn more about this or to see some other applications, you can check out Andrej Karpathy's blog. He posts a lot about automatic text generation in terms of:

Baby names

Linux source code

Algebraic geometry

Wikipedia articles

Shakespeare

Paul Graham essays

Automatic Handwriting Generation

This task has provided a corpus of examples of handwriting and generates new handwriting for a certain phrase or word. The handwriting is given as coordinate sequences used by a pen once the samples have been created. From the body, the connection of the letters and the pen movement is learned and the new examples are able to be created ad hoc.

Internet Search

Chances are when you hear the word search; your first thought is Google. But there are actually several other search engines out there such as duckduckgo, AOL, Ask, Bing, and Yahoo. Every search engine out there uses some form of a data science algorithm to provide their users the best results for their search query in less than a second. Think about this. Google process over 20 petabytes of data every single day. If there wasn't any data science, Google would not be as good as it is today.

Image Recognition

Another big area of use for deep learning is with image recognition. This tool is used to identify and recognize objects and people in images and to better understand the context and content. This tool has already been used in many sectors such as tourism, retail, social media, gaming, and so on.

The task will require the objects' classification that is in a certain picture as one of a set of objects that it already knew. A complex version of this would be object detection which involves identifying more than one object in a scene of photo and placing a box around it.

Automatic Image Caption Generation

This task is where a certain image is provided and the system has to come up with a caption that describes what is in the photo. In 2014, a boom of deep learning algorithms achieved pretty big results when it came to this problem. It leveraged the work from top models in order to classify and detect objects in pictures.

After an object has been detected in a photo and it has generated the labels for the object, you will be able to see that the following step would be to change those labels into a coherent descriptive sentence.

Typically, this system will involve using large convolutional neural networks in order to detect the object in a photo and will then use a RNN, such as a LSTM, to change the label into something coherent.

Automatic Colorization

This is the process of adding color to photos that were originally black and white. Deep learning is able to use the objects and the content of the photo to color these images, a lot like how a human operator would approach something like this. The capability leveraged the large convolutional neural networks and great quality that is created for ImageNet and co-opted to help solve the issue of this task.

Typically, this approach will mean that there are a large convolutional neural network and many layers that will provide you with the colored image.

This was traditionally performed by hand by humans because of the difficulty of the task.

Advertising

Advertising, another big area that has been changed by the advent of deep learning, has been used by advertisers and publishers to up the relevancy of ads and to boost their ROI of their campaigns. For example, deep learning helps publishers and ad networks to leverage the content so that they can create precisely targeted display advertising, real-time bidding for their ads, data-driven predictive advertising, and many more.

Recommender Systems

Think about the suggestions Amazon gives you. They help you find relevant products from billions of others, but that also improve your experience. There are a lot of companies out there that use this system to promote suggestions that align with their user's internet. The giants of the internet like IMDB, LinkedIn, Netflix, Google Play, Twitter, Amazon, and several more use this type of system to make their user's experience better. The recommendations you see are based upon your previous searches.

Predicting Earthquakes

There was a Harvard scientist that figured out how to use deep learning to teach a computer system to perform viscoelastic computations. These are the computations that are used to predict earthquakes. Until they figured this out, these types of computations were computer intensive, but the deep learning application helped improve calculations by 50,000%. When we are talking about earthquake calculation, timing plays a large and important role. This improvement may just be able to save a life.

Neural Networks for Brain Cancer Detection

A French research team found that finding invasive brain cancer cells while in surgery was hard, mainly because of the lighting in the OR. They discovered that when they used neural networks along with Raman spectroscopy during surgery, it allowed them to detect the cancer cells more easily and lowered the leftover cancer. Actually, this is only a single piece of many over the last couple of months that have matched the workings of advanced classification and recognition with several kinds of cancers and screening tools.

Neural Networks in Finances

Futures markets have been extremely successful since they were created in both developing and developed countries over the last few decades. The reason for it succeeding is due to the leverage futures provide for people who are participants in the market. They examined the trading strategy, which did better because of the leverage by using cost-of-carry relationship and CAPM. The team would then apply the technical trading rules that had been created from spot market prices, on futures market prices that used a hedge ratio based on CAPM. The historical price data of 20 stocks from all of the 10 markets are a part of the analysis.

Automatic Game Playing

This task involves a model of learning how to play a computer-based game using only the pixels that are on the screen. This is a pretty hard task in the realm of deep reinforcement models, which has also been a breakthrough for DeepMind, which was part of Google. Google DeepMind's AlphaGo has expanded and culminated in this.

Activision-Blizzard, Nintendo, Sony, Zynga, and EA Sports have been the leaders in the gaming world and brought it to the next level through data science. Games are now being created by using machine learning algorithms which are able to upgrade and improve playing as the player moves through the game. When you are playing a motion game, the computer analyzes the previous moves to change the way the game performs.

Conclusion

Thank for making it through to the end of *Deep Learning*. Let's hope it was informative and able to provide you with all of the tools you need to achieve your goals whatever they may be.

The next step is to use what you have learned in this book and apply it to your work. Deep learning has a lot of great tools that can help improve any business that uses data. While it may sound confusing or difficult at first, once you get used to it, it makes life a lot easier.

Finally, if you found this book useful in any way, a review on Amazon is always appreciated!

Book 2

Artificial Intelligence

How Artificial Intelligence Works
and How We Apply Artificial
Intelligence to Harness Its Power for
Our Future

Introduction

Congratulations on downloading *Artificial Intelligence* and thank you for doing so.

Artificial Intelligence is a field that has a long history but has continued to grow and change. It is a powerful driving force in changing humanity by assisting businesses and people generate exciting, creative products and services, make critical decisions, and attain major goals. This is the reason why organizations keep hiring AI experts at a jaw-dropping speed.

The median salary of an AI developer in the US is not less than $80,000 based on payscale.com. Virtually all great tech companies run an artificial intelligence project and are ready to cash out millions of dollars to assist in completing the project.

Approximately 13.6 million jobs will emerge in the AI field in the next decade. However, there is a staggering shortage of talent in AI. For example, there are less than 10,000 people in the world with the skill set sufficient to carry out a significant research.

Artificial Intelligence (AI) technology is highly popular in our daily lives. It has applications in different sectors right from gaming, media to finance, and also the state-of-the-art research industries from medical diagnosis, robotics, and quantum science. The Artificial Intelligence Book for beginners focuses on driving an interest in its learners in the field of AI so that they are ready to learn more advanced topics in the same field.

The introduction to AI explains the background history of artificial intelligence, robotics, learning methods of Artificial Intelligence, basics of modern AI, and some representative of applications of AI. Along the way, we also plan to excite you about the huge possibilities in the field of AI, which continues to drive human ability beyond our imagination.

Chapter 1: Background to Artificial Intelligence

Can Machines Think Like We Humans?

The first part of the 20th century was the time when science fiction started to introduce the concept of artificially intelligent robots. This began with the "Tin Man" from the Wizard of Oz and went on with the impersonated Maria Metropolis.

When the 1950s arrived, there already was a crop of scientists, philosophers, and mathematicians with the idea of artificial intelligence penetrated into their minds.

One example of this person is a young British polymath called Alan Turing who said that human beings make use of existing information to reason and solve problems. And so, machines can also do the same. This illustrated his logic in a paper dated 1950 called "Computing Machinery and Intelligence" which explained how one can create intelligent machines and measure their intelligence too.

Make Pursuit Possible

Unfortunately, it is very easy and cheap to speak. Turing couldn't implement this concept during that time. Well, some of the reasons which stopped Turing from putting his idea into action include a need for computers to change. If you were to trace back and look at the 1949 computers, there were many improvements and discoveries which are required to be done.

These computers lacked the fundamental element of intelligence. It was very hard to instruct this computer to execute any command. In short, the 1950s computers couldn't send commands to implement or remember whatever they did. Secondly, computing was not cheap but very expensive. For example, the cost of hiring a computer was around $200, 000 per month. Only the biggest universities and large tech companies could afford to spend such a huge amount of money. The need to prove a concept and effort from highly influential people is what was needed to convince funding sources that Artificial Intelligence was a great field worth to pursue.

The Conference that Sounded the Bell

After five years, evidence to support the concept of Artificial Intelligence was realized through Allen Newell, Herbert Simon, and Cliff Shaw's Logic Theorist. This was a program which had been designed with the aim to emulate how to solve problems of a human being and get funding from the Research and Development Corporation. Many see it as the first program of artificial intelligence that was presented at the Dartmouth Summer Research Project on Artificial Intelligence that was hosted by John McCarthy and Marvin Minsky.

In this conference, McCarthy united top researchers from different fields and allowed them to have an open-ended discussion on Artificial Intelligence which was used at the same event. Unfortunately, this conference didn't live up to McCarthy's expectations. People came and walked away as they pleased and they did not agree on standard methods for the field. However, everyone who attended was in agreement with the statement that AI is achievable. This was only the most positive thing from this conference. But the importance of this event could not be ignored because it triggered research into AI.

The Road to Success and Setbacks

Between 1957 and 1974, AI rapidly developed. Computers were designed that had the ability to store a lot of information and process information faster. New machine learning algorithms were developed and people got enlightened to know which type of algorithm to choose to solve their problem.

Examples by Newell and Simon's General Problem Solver were great examples to show the goals of problem-solving and interpretation of spoken language. Such success and the advocacy by top researchers made the government agencies to begin to fund in Artificial Intelligence research. The government was very interested in a machine that could transcribe and translate spoken language.

In 1970, Marvin Minsky talked to Life Magazine and predicted that three to eight years from then, there will be a machine that has the general intelligence of an average human being. While there was a basic proof of concept, the journey was still long before this could be achieved.

To achieve AI, there were several obstacles experienced. The biggest problem was the lack of a computational power to execute anything significant. For example, computers didn't store enough information and process it fast. For communication to take place, it was important to understand the definition and meaning of words. Hans Moravec was McCarthy's doctoral student during that time, he stated the following "computers were still millions of times too weak to exhibit intelligence." People started to lose patience and this then affected the funding, and soon research slowed down for about ten years.

Later in the 1980s, AI was brought to the limelight by two sources. One included the extension of the algorithmic toolkit and a raise of funds. Both Rumelhart and John Hopfield were the key people who started to spread the idea of "deep learning" techniques that created room for computers to learn by experience.

Conversely, Edward Feigenbaum created an expert system with the ability to mimic the decision-making process of a human expert.

The program could ask an expert how to respond to a particular situation, and once this was learned for virtually every incidence, people who are not experts could gain advice from a program. Expert systems were largely used in industries.

The Japanese government accorded a lot of support to expert systems and other advances in AI developments. Between 1982-1990, the Japanese invested $400 million dollars with the focus to revolutionize computer processing, implement a logic program, and enhance artificial intelligence. However, the set goals were not achieved. But one can argue that the indirect effects of Fifth Generation Computer Project inspired the talented young generation of engineers and scientists.

Even with the lack of government funding, AI did not die. In fact, between 1990 and 2000, many goals of artificial intelligence were achieved. In 1997, the world chess champion was defeated by a computerized chess program. This highly popularized match was the first time that a world chess champion had been defeated by a computer chess program. This was a big step towards the creation of an artificially intelligent decision-making program.

In the same period, other developments were also witnessed such as a speech recognition program created by Dragon Systems. This program was installed and run on windows. This was another big step realized in the field of spoken language interpretation. Soon, it seemed like there was no problem which machines couldn't solve. For example, emotions of human beings were illustrated by the Kismet robot. This robot had the ability to detect and show human emotions.

Time is the Healer of All Wounds

Still, how artificial intelligence could be programmed was a nightmare. So what might have changed? Well, it turns out that the biggest computer storage limitation which seemed to prevent researchers 30 years ago was not at all a problem. For example, it was approximated that the memory and speed of computers doubled each year. This is actually how Deep Blue eclipsed Garry Kasparov in 1997. It is the same way in which Google's Alpha Go defeated Chinese Go champion, Kie Je. This seems to explain the roller coaster of AI research.

Artificial Intelligence is Everywhere

As of today, we are in the era of "big data, "a time when humans have the ability to gather big sums of information that is impossible for a human being to process. The application of artificial intelligence has been a significant success in many industries like entertainment, marketing, and banking. Although algorithms can't do a lot, both big and massive computing will facilitate artificial intelligence to learn using brute force.

Top Example Application of Artificial Intelligence

Artificial Intelligence and Quantum Computing

The fact is that no one can stop AI from evolving. Humans have continued to focus on enhancing life across each spectrum, and the application of technology has turned out to be an engine for achieving that. While the past 100 years might be seen as the most dramatic technological upheavals to life compared to all human history, the coming 100 years are going to create a way for the multi-generational.

This shall be at the hands of Artificial Intelligence which has become smarter, more-fluid, and faster because of Quantum computing. The Quantum computers have been designed to solve life's most complex challenges and mysteries related to aging, poverty, war, famine, and many other things.

Beyond the application of Quantum-computing, the current A.I systems have advanced machine learning programs with massive behavioral algorithms which suit themselves to the likes and dislikes. Although it is largely useful, these machines aren't going to get smarter in an existential way, but they shall enhance their skills and usefulness depending on the dataset.

There are a few popular examples of artificial intelligence being applied today. For example:

1. Siri

If you are a lover of Apple, then you must be familiar with Siri — a personal assistant. She has a friendly voice that she uses to interact with users daily. She helps Apple users discover information, give directions, add events to their calendars, send messages, and many other things. In short, Siri is a pseudo-intelligent digital personal assistant. She applies machine learning technology to respond to users.

2. Alexa

Alexa shocked many when it emerged to become the smart home's hub. Introduced and created by Amazon. One of its strongest unique ability is to decipher speech from any place in the room, set alarms, schedule appointments, and also power smart homes.

3. Tesla

If you don't have a Tesla, then you have no clue what you are missing. This is one of the best cars that have ever been designed. Not because many people have expressed the beauty of the vehicle but its predictive ability, self-driving features and the technological "coolness" it brings. If you are into cars, then you need to go get an experience of Tesla cars.

4. Cogito

This is one of the best examples of behavioral adaptation to help enhance the emotional intelligence of customer support representatives found on the market today. The company is an integration of machine learning and behavioral science to boost customer interaction for phone professionals.

5. Boxever

This is a company which deals a lot with machine learning to help enhance the experience of the customer in the travel industry and supply micro-moments that satisfies customers along the way. It is via machine learning and application of A.I that the company has domineered the playing field. This helps customers to discover new methods of engaging their customers in the playing field.

6. Netflix

Netflix has an advanced predictive technology depending on customer's reactions to films. It will analyze billions of records to recommend films which you might like depending on the previous choices and reactions to films. This tech is increasingly getting smarter every year as the size of the dataset increases.

Chapter 2: Robotics

Nearly everywhere you go now you'll see Artificial Intelligence implemented. On the screens, pockets, and who knows maybe one day it might be walking to a home near you. The headlines tend to strike this extensive field into a single subject. Robots being developed from labs, algorithms playing traditional games and winning, AI and some of the things which it can achieve are becoming part of our everyday lives. Although most of these incidences have a specific link to AI, this is not at all a monolithic field, but one that has many different disciplines.

Artificial intelligence and photonics have made it possible to develop robots using new methods of linking business, medicine, and many other applications. There is no argument that the age of robot has come upon us. The idea of robots might bring to mind important androids such as C-3PO in "Star Wars" and Rosie from "The Jetsons". It might even send fears to human beings because advanced robots continue to become better and indispensable. Most of these robots have now assumed dangerous or boring jobs done by human beings. Whichever the case, many people haven't come to realize the ubiquitous nature of robots because, in many incidences, the robots are less Android and resemble industrial tools. Integrating photonics technology such as sensors, lasers, and facial recognition technology, robotics exist in every field starting from industrial processing devices like Google's self-driving car.

Based on the International Federation of Robotics (IFR), the year 2013 witnessed an increased sale of industrial robots in the chemical, automotive, and food processing industries. The automotive sector contains one-third of all industrial robots that help in car manufacturing. IFR estimates that between 2012 and 2013, the global call for personal and domestic service robots increased to $1.7 billion.

The classic nature of robots has resulted in a huge progress too. For instance, when it was announced that a hotel in Japan would be provided with a human-like robot, the concept of fleshy humanoid robots from the "Future World" or "Westworld" started to become a reality.

The "Henn-na Hotel in Nagasaki Prefecture", translated to "Strange Hotel" was to be supplied with receptionist robots that have a strong human likeness. These robots had to greet visitors and involve them in intelligent conversations. Robots were also to provide room service, housekeeping, and porter service.

Another robot that is less human and more logical is the Baxter series of robots at Rethink Robotics Inc. in Boston. Baxter has a good interactive platform that combines 360 sonar sensors and personalized software. Baxter operates even though there are great workers who can optimize the research and manufacturing process. Baxter's camera support application of computer vision using a 30-fps image capture rate and great resolution of 640 x 400 pixels.

During the launch of the Australian Centre for Robotic Vision, Sue Keay, the chief operating officer at ACRV said that the robotic vision is main technology which will support robotics to transform labor-intensive industries and obstruct with stagnating markets. This will then turn robots into a ubiquitous feature of the current world.

That being said, let's learn some deep concepts about robotics. So, what do you think is a robot? Well, you can pick any definition which you think is right for you, but we shall define a robot as "a device which performs work." And I guess you know what work is. If not, work is the exertion of energy. As you can see, the definition of a robot is open to anything that is non-human.

We aren't going to judge whether the robot is going to perform an important task. How important the robot is can be determined by the creator. And your robot doesn't need to have two legs which it can walk for it to be considered a robot.

Now you can see that at one point in your life, you have used robots but didn't realize that. For example, a vending machine is a great example of a robot. Other examples include a washing machine and dishwasher. Don't forget the automatic checkout lane found in a grocery. In other words, robots are always around us and you aren't supposed to fear them.

The function of a robot is to perform a given a task. So it should always have a means in which it can execute tasks. The technique to complete a task arises from its controlling mechanism and structure.

The Structure

The structure refers to the physical components. A robot can have one or more physical parts that assume a specific motion to perform a task. Take the example of a vending machine. It contains motorized spiral things which push the product out. The dishwasher contains a water-spraying arm that sprays water on the dishes. A washing machine contains motor which rotates the drum that holds clothes.

Control

For an action to take place, the structure must have control. Your robot will remain in one position unless you provide a control technique. The vending machine has a control panel that will let a customer pay for a given product. Dishwasher and washing machine have control panels and buttons. If you look at the automatic checkout lane, it contains a touchscreen control with an interface.

Types of Control

Robots have two types of control. There is the external control and internal control. For robots that are controlled externally, there is a different entity which seems to control it. On the other hand, internally controlled robots are autonomous. This means that it controls itself. As such, its controller is located inside the structure. The controller decides what steps or actions to do next on its own without any interference. For the external control, there are power switches and various configuration buttons. But once the internally-controlled robot is on, it performs the work on its own without any human interference.

Humanoid robots such as Honda's Asimo are autonomous. For the autonomous robots, there should be a means to detect their environment before decisions are made. This means that they have one sensor. Still, every autonomous robot can have different types of microcontroller installed inside. Many but not all externally controlled robots have a microcontroller inside. There are various types of microcontrollers that have different names. Usually, it keeps changing. At the center of a microcontroller, you will find a microprocessor core.

Popular cores are found in many products and have many followers. By learning how to program popular cores, it can give you a great opportunity to land a job in programming with a reputed company. For that reason, developers and programmers for popular cores are in high demand.

The core microprocessor is the main structure in the internal controller. The controller may not run a function if it doesn't have a software. Your robot's software could be predetermining.

153

This means that you might not require to program it. But you may need to configure it by setting up some input switches before you control your robot with an external controller.

Now that you have learned some basic about robots, you can begin to think about how you can use this knowledge to even learn more.

Artificial Intelligence and Robots

In the first two decades of the 21st century, there has been an expansion of 'autonomous technology' and 'artificial intelligence'. Drones, self-driving cars, space exploration, software agents, and deep learning in medical diagnosis are among the most popular examples of areas where artificial intelligence has redefined. Artificial Intelligence in the form of machine learning and the presence of extensive datasets are some of the life domains which have driven development.

The unification of these digital technologies has even made them more powerful. AI installed in these systems can help redefine or improve conditions for humans and reduce the need for human contribution and interference during operation. Therefore, it is replacing humans with smart technology in hard, dirty, boring, and dangerous work.

Without any direct human intervention and external control, smart systems can facilitate dialogue with customers in online call-centers, drive robot hands to choose and manipulate objects accurately, purchase and sell stock at large quantities in a twinkle of an eye.

Despite this, it is sad that some of the most powerful cognitive tools are mostly opaque.

Their actions aren't programmed by humans in a linear sequence. Google Brain designs AI which presumably builds AI better than human beings.

Chapter 3: Reinforcement Learning

Reinforcement learning is one of those topics that is widely discussed, contemplated, and researched in Artificial Intelligence because it has the ability to change most businesses. This section will look at reinforcement learning and further provide some practical examples of areas where it is used today.

What is Reinforcement Learning?

At the heart of reinforcement learning is the idea that the maximum behavior or action is enhanced by a positive reward.

Just like toddlers who begin to learn to walk have to adjust actions depending on the results they experience like taking a smaller step if the earlier step made them fall or knock something, machines and software agents have reinforcement learning algorithms which help choose the correct behavior depending on the previous feedback from the environment. As you can see, this is another form of machine learning and at the same time a branch of artificial intelligence.

Going by the complexity and nature of the problem, algorithms created for reinforcement learning can continue to adapt to the environment over time to take advantage of the reward in the long-term. Similar to the teetering toddler, a robot that is attempting to learn how to walk using reinforcement learning will attempt different ways to fulfill the objective, and receive feedback about how successful those methods are and then adjust until that point when the purpose to walk is realized. Making a big step forward causes the robot to fall, so it can adjust its step to ensure that it is smaller to test whether that is the way of maintaining stability.

It can proceed with learning through making different small steps until it is able to walk. In this case, the end reward is to stay upright, while the punishment is to fall. Depending on the feedback, the robot actions are reinforced.

Reinforcement learning requires a lot of data, and that is the reason why first applications in this technology have fields where simulated data is easily available.

Definitions of Reinforcement Learning

You can understand reinforcement learning by applying the idea of actions, agents, environments, and rewards. You will learn more about these terms shortly.

Capital letters represent a set of items and the lower-case letters denote an instance of a particular thing. For example, A describes all possible actions which represent a particular action in a set.

- **Agent**: An **agent** will select an action.

- **Action (A):** A is the set of all possible moves the agent can create.

- **Discount Factor:** This is multiplied by the agent to dampen the following rewards on choice of the agent's action.

- **Environment:** It describes the surrounding environment of the agent. Environment will accept the present state of the agent and action as input. The output is the reward of the agent and the next state.

- **State (S):** This describes the immediate situation that the agent discovers itself. This could be a specific moment and place.

- **Reward (R):** It is the feedback you can use to gauge the failure or success of an agent's actions.

- **Policy:** It is an approach which an agent uses to define the next action depending on the present state. It combines states to actions, the actions that have the best rewards.

- **Value (V):** It is the long-term return outcome that is expected instead of the short-term reward R.

- **Q-Value:** Resembles value but it has an additional parameter.

- **Trajectory:** Describes a sequence of actions and states that affect those states.

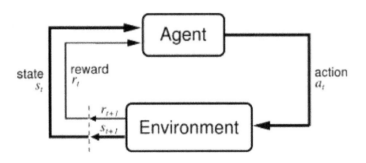

The feedback loop indicated above subscript refers to time steps t and t + 1. Each subscript explains various states. We have the current state t and t + 1. While other categories of machine learning such as supervised and unsupervised learning can be trained based on the state-action pairs, reinforcement learning determines actions based on the results it displays. In other words, it is a goal-oriented type of learning that learns a series of actions that make an agent achieve a particular goal.

Additionally, the difference between reinforcement learning and other types of learning-supervised and unsupervised learning is based on the way it interprets inputs.

- Unsupervised learning: The algorithm will learn similarities and through extension, it can sport the inverse and carry out any anomaly detection by identifying any unusual thing.

- Supervised learning: This is where the algorithm will learn corrections between instances of data and their labels.

- Reinforcement learning: This is where actions depend on short and long-term rewards.

Domain Selection for Reinforcement Learning

One approach which you can use to understand more about autonomous reinforcement learning agent is to imagine a person who is blind trying to walk around the world with ears and a white cane. The agents have a small room which gives them a chance to respond to their surroundings. However, this room may not be the best technique for them to identify whatever that is around them.

Additionally, to make a choice between the type of feedback and input which your agent has to deal with is a great challenge. Algorithms that are trained to play video games can skip this problem because of the environment.

As a result, video games create a sterile environment of the lab. This is the right time to test concepts on reinforcement learning. The human mind is a prerequisite domain selection, especially on matters about theories and knowledge of a given problem that should be solved.

The State-Action Pairs and Complex Probability Distribution

The goal of reinforcement learning is to select the best action for any particular state. In this case, actions are ranked and allocated values. Since the majority of the actions depend on a given state, you therefore need to measure the value of the state-action pairs.

This means that actions should be ranked and assigned values relative to each other. Since most of these actions depend on the state, what you are supposed to measure is the value of state-action pairs.

With reinforcement learning, you get the chance to model a complex probability distribution reward with respect to a massive state-action pair. For that reason, this particular type of learning goes hand in hand with a Markov decision process.

Reinforcement learning is iterative. It is commonly used to discover reward state-action pairs.

Machine Learning and Time

An algorithm is a method that you can take to aggregate lessons of time. The reinforcement learning algorithms have a special link to time. An algorithm can use the same state to test different actions until that time when it can attain the best action. Additionally, algorithms have a Groundhog Day where it acts dumb but continue to become wise with time.

Given that human beings have never experienced a Groundhog Day, reinforcement learning algorithms can learn a lot and work better than human beings. Therefore, the advantageous point of these algorithms over human beings is their ability to work parallel.

Deep Reinforcement Learning and Neural Networks

Neural networks are agents which learn to map a specific state-action and pair rewards. Not different to other neural networks, it contains coefficients which estimate the function which associates inputs and outputs.

When it comes to reinforcement learning, you can use convolutional networks to identify an agent's state. This means that it implements the task of image recognition. But convolutional networks run different interpretations from images in the reinforcement learning to supervised learning.

Chapter 4: Computer Vision

To teach a computer to learn how to see is not an easy task. Yes! You can connect a camera on a PC but that won't make it see. For a device to see the world the way people or animals do, it has to rely on computer vision and image recognition.

Therefore, computer vision is the reason why the barcode scanner can identify a set of stripes in a UPC. Additionally, this is how Apple's Face ID can determine whether a face that a camera has captured is yours.

Generally, when a device processes raw visual input like JPEG file, it can use computer vision to understand whatever it is seeing. It is easy for a person to look at computer vision as the part of the human brain that processes information that the eyes receive, rather than the eyes themselves.

An important function of computer vision from the AI perspective is the image recognition which provides the machine with the ability to describe the input received through computer vision and categorize everything that it sees.

Below are examples of image recognition work.

- The eBay application that has a camera to use to search items.

- Facebook's AI knows much about your photos.

- Neural networks changes pitch black photos into bright images.

- An AI program that can read the human mind.

There are also mobile applications which use a camera to determine whether an object is a hotdog or not. An example of this app is the NotHotdog. This app applies computer vision and image recognition to generate judgments. While it may not be a very attractive app, the process of training a neural network to run image recognition is complex both in the human brain and computers.

A computer vision has a sense of sight that is different from that understanding of the physical universe. And that is the reason why training is very important. It is similar to how a child is trained to identify numbers and letters. Children must be shown a number or letter several times so that they can recognize the number.

Still, many kids can quickly recognize numbers and letters while upside down once they can identify it in the upright position. Humans have a strong biological neural network that describes visual information.

The way image recognition works depends on the development of a neural network that processes individual image pixels. Researchers train these networks to allow them to identify similar images.

For instance, in the case of the hotdog, developers can feed an AI program with thousands of hotdog pictures. This particular AI can then develop a general idea of how a picture of a hotdog appears. If you supply it with an image, it has to compare with each pixel of that image with a hotdog image. If the input matches with the pixels of the image, AI defines it as a hot dog.

How AI Recognize an Image

Convolutional Neural Network drives computer vision technology. All data in a computer is read as a series of o and 1. Additionally, it has a wide variety of computational method to display different results. First, let's see how a computer reads an image using the ConvNet.

At one point in our lives, we have been "artists". During this time, we built and drew colored figures by using various shades that have a beautiful texture. The way you can differentiate things with your eyes is by how you perceive color. Consider an example of different colors on the pallet. There are different colors that have been tested and mixed to create a darker, light shade of color depending on the ratio used.

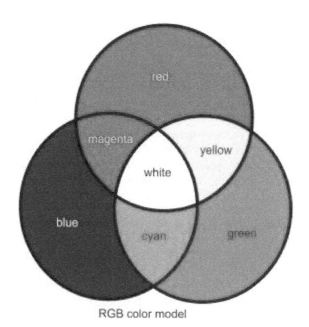

RGB color model

In the same way, Artificial Intelligence reads the above colors with a range of values from 0 to 255. The image above shows how you can apply the combination to remember the six major colors. It is referred to as the RGB model. In this case, Red, Green, and Blue are the dominant colors. Once they are combined together, another set of colors is developed (Cyan, Yellow, and Magenta).

The image below represents an experience. This describes a visual perception which defines white as a mix of different colors.

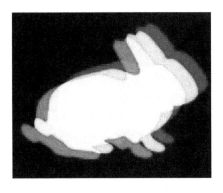

What is Seen by a Computer

Computer images have three important colors — red, blue, and green. There are several models applied in the computer vision field. In this section, you'll be introduced to a simple RGB model which describes how a computer can detect an image.

The RGB model is one of the oldest color differentiation tool found in the computer vision field. Since each major color has a value between 0 -255, a color with a high value implies that it is a brighter color. Next, let's divide each color into a subcategory which generates a color pallet.

Traverse from 0 to 255

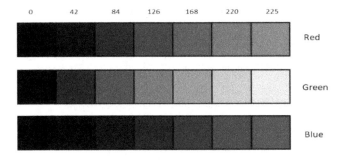

In the above image, each blue, red, and green color represents a particular shade of color. AI uses these numbers to interpret and process the image. When you combine two colors, for example, red and green, the final result is yellow. The yellow color is represented in three-dimensional space such as 255, 255, 0 (R.G.B). And so, RGB makes it possible to look at various colors like Cyan, Yellow, and Magenta.

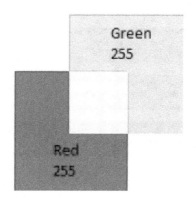

Images are made up of pixels which are close to another. The colored pixels have three channels organized one behind the other. All the channels operate together to display a specific color. Let's see how AI reads an image. If you implement the RGB model, you'll be able to extract more than 16 million shades of colors.

Values of a Pixel in an Image

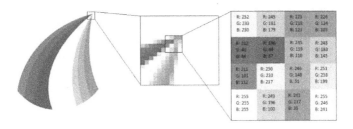

The above image is composed of three channels which are arranged one behind the other. Let's find out how the above channels are arranged to help find a pixelated image such the one shown above.

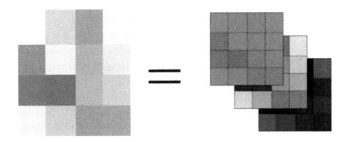

Image Recognition using ConvNet

Given that AI knows the pixel of each image, it can extract the values of RGB and keep it in memory. It begins by searching for a match of images that are similar and found in the database. Well, how is this whole process done?

In ML, ConvNet represents a complex feed-forward neural network. Why it is applied in classification and image recognition is because of the better accuracy.

The ConvNet sticks to a model which operates on creating a network and can send out a complete layer that has all interconnected neurons.

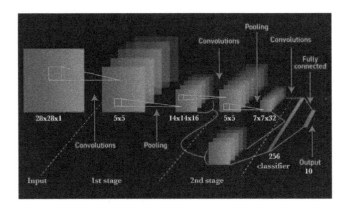

During the process of training of ConvNet, the hidden layer is the point at which the image is broken down. This is referred to as convolution. Each image comprises of an nxm number of pixels with a specific depth. In the ConvNet, the images are divided into two processes. Those two processes include filtering and pooling.

Filtering is the process that results in the transfer of a weight matrix over the entire image in various iterations to help in the calculation of the dot product of the original pixel values and weights.

Typically, this is followed by a layer of pooling which converts the size of an image into a low dimensional matrix.

How Deep Learning Enhances Machine Vision

Digitization has great grip on industrial production with processes automated as part of the industrial Internet of Things (IIOT). When it comes to IIoT also known as Industry 4.0, different machines and robots pick on the majority of everyday production tasks. Take for example in assembly, new, compact and mobile robots like collaborative robots work hand in hand with their human colleagues.

The IIoT's highly automated and universally networked production flow features a machine-to-machine interaction based on the machine vision to correctly identify a wide variety of objects in the flow of goods in factories and the entire chain process. Machine vision improves the efficiency and safety of the above workflows and has become an indispensable device for engineers who want to automate and speed production.

As of today, innovation machine learning and deep learning process have created strong recognition rates. Thanks to the developments in artificial intelligence, companies have the ability to benefit from a higher degree of automation, greater productivity and correct identification, and handling of a wide collection of objects using the whole value chain.

Since the "eye of production", machine vision software has turned to be an important element of technology, processing unstructured data like digital image and video produced by cameras to select objects by their external optical features alone. This particular software works fast and attains a high and reliable identification rate. Additionally, it is applied in a wide range of tasks like fault inspection and automatic handling of objects in robotics.

Analyze and Assess Large Data Sets

In an effort to make sure that the identification process is robust and adaptable to the requirements of networked IIoT processes, machine vision software developers increasingly depend on methods from the branch of artificial intelligence. Deep learning is a branch of machine learning that allows computers to get trained and learn via architectures such as convolutional neural networks (CNN).

The specific feature of AI, deep-learning, and machine-learning technologies is that it is analyzed in detail and evaluate large amounts of data to train a lot of classes and effectively distinguish between objects. Additionally, this particular data is produced within IIoT.

To apply deep learning, CNNs has to be trained. This particular training process associates to specific external features which are typical of the object such as texture, shape, color, and surface structure. The objects are classified into various classes depending on the above properties to assign them more precisely.

Train Objects Using Classification

How exactly does the training process work? The user will first supply image data which has been provided with labels already. Then, every label corresponds to a tag which defines the identity of the specific object. The system shall analyze this particular data, and based on this produce "trains" which are similar to the models of the objects recognized.

As a result of the following self-learned object models, the deep learning network can be able to assign the newly-added image data to the relevant classes like their data content. As such, the items can continue to be recognized automatically.

A simple image for direct comparison is no longer relevant for each individual object. After all, deep learning processes can learn from new things independently. By accepting features of all image data, conclusions can be extracted from properties of a given class, which considerably enhances the identification rates. This process is referred to as "inference."

And so, deep learning algorithms are very good for optical character recognition (OCR) applications that are accurately identifying number or letter combinations. Because of the extensive training process, the general feature of individual characters is exactly identified depending on the classes defined. But because there are a lot of different fonts, others with deviating features like serifs, problems can emerge assigning them with certainty.

Reduce Excessive Training Time

Companies avoid using AI-based technologies like deep learning because of their complexity. They need developers to have a great expertise. The training process usually calls for a lot of sample images to identify objects.

More than 100,000 comparison images might be required for every class to accomplish the right recognition rates. Although the relevant sample data is present, the training process usually picks a huge amount of time. Typically, the programming work for recognizing different defect classes at the time of fault inspection are often complex. The reason is that highly skilled employees with the right training are needed for this purpose.

The modern machine vision solutions that have a large number of deep learning functions can assist. The new version of the standard software MVTec HALCON allows companies to train convolutional neural networks without a great deal of money and time. At the end of the day, the software is installed with two networks which are optimally pre-trained for industrial use.

Therefore, the training process operates only with a few sample images supplied by the customer and they are customized to the customer's exact applications. This generates neural networks which can be accurately compared to the customer's individual requirements.

User companies can highly cut down the amount of programming work required by systematically categorizing new image data and saving time and money. Typically, they don't have any in-depth AI expertise. Companies can involve their current personnel without issues to train the network.

Identify Defects Efficiently

Recognize problems in a time-consuming process because the appearances of defects like tiny scratches on an electronic part can be accurately described in advance. As a result, it is hard to manually launch suitable algorithms which can recognize any conceivable faults depending on sample images. An expert may require to manually see hundreds of thousands of images and programs an algorithm which describes the error as accurately depending on this observation.

Deep learning technologies and CNNs, on the other hand, independently train certain characteristics of defects and accurately define similar problem classes. And so, only 500 sample images are required for each class depending on which technology trains, verify, and therefore, detect the different types of defects classes. The self-learning algorithms help to hugely reduce recognition errors, even though the error quotas for manual programming can be quite high.

Chapter 5: Natural Language Processing

What is it and What is it Used For?

Artificial Intelligence (AI) is transforming how everyone looks at the world. AI "robots" are everywhere. Right from our phones to devices such as Amazon's Alexa, the current world is surrounded by machine learning.

Netflix, Google, video games, and data companies including many others apply AI to help handle large amounts of data. The end result includes insights and analysis that might have been difficult.

There is no surprise when different kinds of businesses are adopting large companies' success by applying AI and jumping on the board. However, not all AI is designed equally in the business sector, even though some types of artificial intelligence are useful than others.

This chapter will look at Natural Language Processing (NLP). This is another type of artificial intelligence that concerns on analyzing the human language to develop insights, create advertisements, assists your text, and more.

Well, Why NLP?

Natural Language Processing is a new technology which powers most types of AI that you always see. NLP is currently being applied in many different sectors and that should show you how important it is. You can think of it this way, every day, human beings speak thousands of words that other human beings interpret to perform different things. At the center, it is just simple communication, but we are aware that words run much deeper. There's a specific context by which human beings derive meaning from everything a person says, whether they mean something with their body language or in the way they describe something. Although NLP doesn't rely on voice inflection, it does derive contextual patterns.

This is the point at which its value increases. Let's apply an example to illustrate how powerful NLP is when it is applied in the practical situation. If you are typing on an iPhone just like the way many of us do daily, you'll see suggestions of words depending on what you are typing and what you always type. And that is called natural language processing in action. It is this little thing that many of us take for granted, and have been ignoring for years, but that is the reason why NLP becomes very important. Now let's bring it to the business world.

Let's say that a company wants to choose how best it can advertise to their users. They can opt to apply Google to identify common search terms which users type when they look for their product.

NLP will support for quick compilation of data into terms which are related to their brand and those that might not expect. Taking advantage of the uncommon terms might provide the company with the ability to advertise in new ways.

Well, How Does NLP Work?

As said above, natural language processing is a type of artificial intelligence which analyzes the human language. It exists in many forms, but at the center, the technology assists machine to understand and communicate with human speech.

However, understanding NLP isn't that straightforward. It is an advanced type of AI that has of late become viable. This means that not only are we just learning about NLP but also it is hard to grasp. The following is a breakdown of NLP in layman's term. This means that it is the easiest way to understand the way natural language processing works.

The first thing in NLP is based on the application of the system. Voice-based systems such as Alexa and Google Assistant have to translate words into text. That is carried out using the Hidden Markov Models system (HMM).

The HMM has math models that allow it to decide whatever you say and translate it into usable NLP system. Break that down, the HMM listens to 10 to 20 milliseconds clips of speech and searches for phonemes to make a comparison with a pre-recorded speech.

The next thing is the actual understanding of the language and context. Every NLP system has a really different technique but on the whole, it is fairly similar. The systems attempt to break every word down into parts of speech.

This often takes place through a series of coded grammar rules which depend on algorithms which incorporate statistical machine learning to assist in determining the context of whatever you speak.

If you are dealing with speech-to-text NLP, the system will skip the first step and jump straight to analyzing words using algorithms and grammar rules. The end result is applied in different ways.

For example, an SEO application might use a coded text to extract keywords related to a specific product.

Semantic Analysis

If you are discussing NLP, it is essential to break down semantic analysis. It is closely associated with NLP and one may even argue that semantic analysis allows the development of the natural language processing.

Semantic analysis refers to how NLP AI can logically interpret human sentences. When the HMM method break sentences down into their standard structure, semantic analysis will permit the process to add content.

For example, if an NLP program searched for the word "DUMMY", it must have the context to check whether the text refers to calling someone "dummy" or it just refers to something else such as car crash.

When the HMM method breaks down the text and NLP supports the formation of human-to-computer communication, then semantic analysis offers room for everything to make sense contextually. Without the presence of semantic analysts, then AI could not have reached the current level.

Problems

The two major problems experienced in the natural language processing include:

1. The level of vagueness in natural languages.

2. The complex nature of semantic information existing in simple sentences.

Normally, language processors have to handle a large number of words, most of which have other alternative application and large grammar which supports the development of different types of phrases. Tools which process language are very complex because of the different types of vagueness and measure of irregularity.

Activities Involved in Natural Language Processing

A simple structure of NLP deals with four major stages. In an actual system, these stages don't take place as different, sequential processes. In this case, both syntactic analysis and semantic analysis are dealt with the same principle.

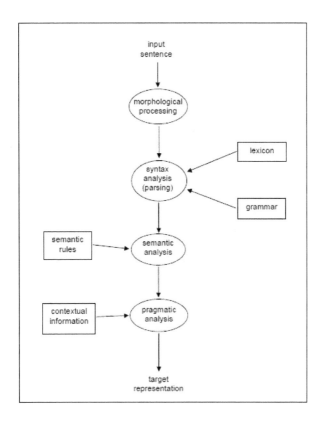

Morphological Processing

The focus of morphological processing is to divide strings of language input into a set of token that resembles discrete words, punctuation forms, and sub-words.

For example, a phrase like "unreal" is divided into two sub-word tokens such as un-real.

Morphology deals with selecting base words to create other words with the same meaning but different syntactic category. The modification takes place by adding a prefix and postfix but other textual changes can take place. Essentially, there are different word cases which lead to modification. That is inflection, derivation, and compounding.

A typical structure of morphological processing depends on the language being analyzed. This means that single words contain all information about the number of sentences, person, and tense. Other languages, this kind of information may spread across different words. For example, the English phrase "I will have been walking" contains a complex tense by just checking at the structure of the auxiliary verbs. Other languages link prefixes to nouns to indicate their roles while other words have inflections to display the proximity of information.

The English is very easy to apply morphological analysis and tokenize than other languages. These languages can have an ambiguous morphology that is resolved by performing semantic and syntactic analysis on the input. An example in English can be between plural and singular verbs.

The result from a morphological process consists of a phase of string tokens which you can apply for lexicon lookup. The tokens may contain gender, number, tense, and in some instances, it may have additional syntactic information for the parser. The next step of processing is called syntax analysis.

Syntax and Semantics

The device that deals with language processing has to perform several functions based on syntax and semantic analysis. The purpose of syntax analysis is to determine that a string of words is accurate and divide it into a structure which reveals the syntactic relation between words.

There is a tool called syntactic analyzer that performs the following with the help of a dictionary of word and a collection of syntax rules. A simplified lexicon might consist of syntactic classification of each word and a simple grammar. The example below includes a simple grammar and lexicon.

Lexicon	
brown	category
cat	Noun
chased	Verb
large	Adjective
rat	Noun
the	Article

Grammar
Sentence → Nounphrase, Verbphrase
Verbphrase → Verb, Nounphrase
Nounphrase → Article, Noun
Nounphrase → Article, Adjective, Noun

Semantic and Pragmatics

The next stage includes pragmatics. Semantics and pragmatics are different. However, there is no universal difference between the two. Semantic analysis is mostly related to the meaning of words, while pragmatic analysis handles the outcome of a semantic analysis. For that reason, if you have a sentence like

"The large cat chased the rat" in semantic analysis can reveal an expression that means a cat but it can't explain more steps to help recognize the cat. That remaining part is left for pragmatic analysis. In other words, the task of pragmatic analysis is to disambiguate sentences that can't be fully disambiguated in the process of semantic and syntactic analysis.

How NLP is Changing Search and Customer Service

So far, you must have interacted with different virtual assistants such as Alexa and Siri. These have been designed to enhance customer service and automate specific tasks. Natural language processing is making artificial intelligence easy to communicate. In this section, you will learn these robots are redefining the customer service.

When Apple launched Siri for iPhone 4S in 2011, it was just a matter of time before other industries realized that speaking to our phones would change both the way we look for information online, plus how we interact with other devices.

However, most users were surprised in the way they used voice-recognition devices.

Voice-activated devices have become the new normal. In a study by the PWC, it indicated that consumers between the ages of 18 to 24 see themselves as "heavy-users" of NLP technology plus 57% of those above 50. And these users don't just chat with their devices but also use them to make purchase decisions. The NPD group discovered that purchasing an Echo, consumers could spend extra money on Amazon.

So what can companies do to ensure that they can be found by Siri? Let's look at the facts based on the Apricot Law's Tom Desmond. Traditionally, customers who used Google were presented with various pages and page results. However, voice assistants only presented one or two options.

But AI platforms attempt to respond to these queries in a human way, and they apply the text of pages in search results to do it. As a result, it is important for content to be optimized for a conversational language with a correct, clear grammatically answers to a particular question such as what, who, when, and why?

Building landing pages with a clear location have become very important than ever in the era of NLP and voice search.

Chatbots

Chatbots get a bad perception just because they are known as smooth female voices which prevent us from speaking to real human beings. However, many popular brands use Chatbots to elevate their customer service to the next level. For instance, Starbucks has applied AI to create a virtual barista. The My Barista app makes use of NLP technology to help users both order coffee through chatbot and predict what customers may want to order in future.

Google Duplex

Google introduced Duplex this year as a robot which has been designed to interact in a natural conversation.

Chapter 6: Recommendation System

We live in an era defined by the shift from traditional industries to an economy based on information technology. Thanks which are aware of the importance of the information they gather in a natural way.

This type of transformation doesn't take place without its own difficulties. For instance, each year the amount of information produced increases exponentially. About 90% of the data around the world has been created in the last two years.

This is about 2.5 quintillion bytes each day. That is 25 followed by 17 zeros every single day. While the world continues to be connected with the ever-increasing number of electronic devices, this amount of daily created data is set to increase in the coming years. If you are confronted with these massive amounts of information, any team of human analysts would be correctly overpowered. So what can organizations and companies do to take advantage of their valuable information?

One of the most recurring issues which have become very popular is how to decide the interest of customers in different contexts. When a company would want to sell a high volume of a specific product to a given audience, it has to dedicate its focus to the right group of customer. This is not simple, and that is noticed when you consider the number of users and products alongside the type of interactions that they might have. For instance, how is it possible to identify the type of items that are the best for a new user or how you can recommend products if there are no ratings?

Traditionally, just general and simple strategies were applied depending on factors such as gender, geographical location, and age. But these rules fail to include the value of the large information present about customers and products. It is not sensible to expect humans to scan through every single combination, something that may take decades. And so, the question stands, what should be done?

What is a Recommendation Engine?

Also known as recommender systems, its popularity started to rise in the retail industry, especially in online retail for customized product recommendations. One of the most popular applications is the Amazon's section on

"Customer who bought this item also bought..." Recommender system refers to a smart and complex salesman who knows the taste and style of the customer. As such, it can make intelligent decisions focused on recommendations that would excite most the customer.

While it first started with e-commerce, it is now widely applied in many different areas. Examples include YouTube's "Recommended Videos" and Netflix's "Other Movies You May Enjoy." Other markets which have started to apply recommendation engines include the transportation industry. Here, IBM uses its control systems.

Essentially, what a recommendation engine does is to filter the data by applying different algorithms and predict the most important product to customers. The first thing is that it had to record the past actions of a customer and based on that recommend products which users might be interested to buy.

In case new users visit an e-commerce site, there will be no previous history of the user. In this case, the recommender system may opt to suggest the best-selling products to the customer. These are the kinds of products that most users buy when they come to the site. Another way is to recommend products which would produce the highest profit to the business. Being able to suggest different items to a customer based on their interests may develop a positive impact on the user. This has the benefit to make the customer make frequent visits to the same site.

As a result, many businesses are installing smart and intelligent recommendation engines by taking into consideration the behaviors of their users.

1. Data collection

The first step when it comes to building a recommender system is a data gathering process. The data can be gathered in two ways — implicit and explicit. Explicit data refers to that which is generated intentionally such as input from users and ratings of a movie. When data is implicit, it means the information is not presented deliberately but gathered from existing streams of data like order history, search history, and clicks.

2. Data Storage

The size of data will define the effectiveness of a recommendation model. For example, in a movie recommender system, the higher the ratings from a user, the better the recommendations become. This specific data is important in making a decision related to the type of storage applied. This specific storage consists of a standard SQL database and other types of storage objects.

3. Filtering data

Once you have collected and stored data, the next thing is to filter it so that you can get the correct information required to form the last suggestions. There are different types of an algorithm that you can use to make the filtering process easy. Below is a description of each algorithm.

Content-based filtering

Also known as cognitive filtering, it recommends items after comparing the user history and the content items. The content of every object is shown as a set of descriptors. The profile of the user is represented using similar terms and build by performing an analysis of items done by the user.

A few things have to be underlined while creating a content-based filtering system. The terms have to be automatically or manually located and a method selected to extract the terms from items.

Next, representing the terms such that is possible to compare the user profile and item correctly. Thirdly, the learning algorithm is chosen to learn and recommend items depending on the user profile.

How to choose a learning method?

The effectiveness of a learning method plays a critical role when it comes to choosing the method to apply. The most important thing is the nature of the complexity of the algorithm.

Storage requirements can be a major challenge since many user histories have to be maintained. Neural and genetic algorithms are usually slower than other learning methods. One reason is that iterations are needed to define whether a document is important. Instance-based methods reduce in effectiveness when a lot of training example is available. Some of the best to use include relevance feedback and Bayesian classifier.

The probability of a learning method to emulate the changes depending on the user's history is important. It is important for the method to assess the training data because instances last for a short time.

Collaborative filtering

It is also known as social filtering. In this approach, information is filtered using recommendations of other people. The major focus revolves around the concept that people who settled on the evaluation of specific items in the past are likely to come to an agreement in the future. An individual who wants to look at a movie, for instance, may ask for a recommendation from friends. The recommendations of some friends who share similar interests are more trusted compared to a recommendation from others. This type of information is applied to the type of movie to watch.

Neighborhood-based approach

Most collaborative filtering systems use the neighborhood-based approach. In this technique, different users are selected based on their similarity to the active user. A prediction for the active user is generated by computing a weighted average of the ratings of the chosen users.

To demonstrate how a collaborative filtering system can make a recommendation, consider the example of ratings in a movie table shown below. This table contains ratings of five movies by five people. A "+" shows that the person loved the movie and a "- "shows that the person did not like the movie.

To predict whether Ken would love the movie "Fargo", a comparison of Ken's ratings with others is done. In this situation, the ratings of Ken and Mike are similar and since Mike loved

Fargo, one can predict that Ken would love the move too.

Movie ratings

	Amy	Jef	Mike	Chris	Ken
The Piano	−	−	+		+
Pulp Fiction	−	+	+	−	+
Clueless	+		−	+	−
Cliffhanger	−	−	+	−	+
Fargo	−	+	+	−	?

Rather than just waiting on the most similar person, a prediction is determined based on the weighted average of recommendations of different people. The weight assigned to a person is defined by the correlation between the people for whom to define a prediction. Just as a standard measure of correlation, you can apply the Pearson correlation coefficient.

Selecting neighborhoods

Most collaborative systems must be able to deal with a large number of users. Predicting something by using thousands of ratings by other people has grave effects on performance. As a result, if the number of users rises up to a certain number, then a selection of the best neighbors has to be performed. In this case, two techniques which can be used include the correlation-thresholding and best-n-neighbor. The first technique identifies only those neighbors whose correlation is higher than a given threshold.

Sparsity problem

While dealing with a lot of ratings can be a very big problem, systems that deal with few ratings trigger serious issues. This problem happens when the number of items is very large, thus reducing the number that users have rated to a small percentage. In this case, there is a chance that two people have few rated items in common which makes the correlation coefficient less reliable. This is called a sparsity problem. A wide variety of solutions have been designed to deal with this problem.

- **Implicit ratings.** There are systems such as later extension of GroupLens that attempt to increase the number of ratings by referencing them from the user's behavior. But still, a user has to identify an item before the system can deduce a rating.

- **Dimensionality reduction.** By cutting down the dimensionality of the information space, the ratings of two users can be applied in making predictions even if they didn't rate the same items.

- **Content description.** By selecting the content of an item instead of the actual item itself, this may increase the size of information that people share. This is a hybrid technique that is used to combine content-based filtering and collaborative filtering.

Item to item approach

This technique is an inversion of the neighborhood-based approach. Rather than measuring the similarities between people, the ratings are applied in measuring the correlation between items. The Pearson correlation coefficient can still be used as a measure. For instance, the ratings of the movies "Fargo" and "Pulp Fiction" have a perfect correlation.

Chapter 7: Internet of Things

All IoT devices need intelligent coordination and control. The last decade saw massive strides made in AI systems, to work together with IoT, no matter the differences.

AI appears to be the most interesting topic nowadays. There are a lot of talks and even misunderstanding and confusion about what AI is precisely and what is not. AI is affecting the current and future industries in the world. It is not running away and is likely to be more relevant as it grows.

The IoT describes ecosystem of discrete computing devices that use sensors connected through internet infrastructure. The idea could be rising up in the industry for some time, but the democratization of computing technology through affordability and availability of small computing devices pushed it to the mainstream.

With an increase in investment, a generation of new products, and the increasing tide of enterprise deployments, artificial intelligence is generating a wave in the Internet of Things (IoT).

Signals

1. The venture capital funding of AI is growing fast.

2. There is a high acquisition of AI focused IoT start-ups.

3. Big organizations across industries are already taking advantage of AI with IoT to supply new offerings and work efficiently.

The AI Key to Opening IoT Potential

Artificial intelligence contributes a big role in IoT applications and deployments. Both acquisitions and investments in startups which integrate AI and IoT have increased in the last two years. Key vendors of IoT platform software now provide combined AI capabilities like machine learning analytics.

The significance of AI in this particular context lies in its potential to rapidly wring insights from data. AI technology, Machine learning, provides the ability to automatically select patterns and identify anomalies in the data that intelligent sensors and devices supply information such as humidity, temperature, vibration, and sound. When compared to the traditional business intelligence devices that track numeric thresholds to be crossed, machine learning approaches can decide operational predictions up to 20 times earlier and with a great accuracy.

Other AI technologies include speech recognition and computer vision can assist in deriving insight from data. AI applications for IoT allow companies to escape unplanned downtime, spawn new products, increase efficiency, and improve risk management.

AI and IOT Working Together

Both AI and IoT have distinct histories but in the same evolution era. All of them started with an aim to boost legacy systems. For the Internet of Things, this refers to automating and improving available infrastructure and processes for better production and efficiency. When it comes to Artificial Intelligence, the original apps were built with a great emphasis on human-centered processes. Nowadays, the move is shifting towards an integrated IoT native and AI-native technique build from the ground ready for transformative digital methods. In most cases, new IoT solutions contain inbuilt features.

Some of the importance and improvements that AI brought include:

1. AI and IoT allow automation which disrupts the labor market by generating a demand for a new and different set of skills in many industries. Some of the industries transformed in the United States by the changing roles include accommodation,

manufacturing, transportation, and food services.

2. AI and IoT are applied in the product to service-oriented business models. IoT provides business leaders with data that they may use to set up intelligent trade-offs. AI provides the intelligence needed to make the choices.

3. AI and IoT create new value propositions.

Role of AI and in the IoT

In the past year, artificial intelligence is a great necessity when you want to build and increase the number of sensor online devices. And it will even be more important when you want to create meaning from the data streamed from the same devices to help IoT revolution.

Quantified Self and IoT Revolution

The phrase "quantified self" makes us understand the start of the combination of IoT and Artificial Intelligence. In other words, quantified self refers to personal knowledge through self-tracking using technology. Are we living a good life? How can you improve it? Where should we save time?

You collect data in many different areas of life. You can analyze inputs such as the quality of air around us. You analyze different states of our mood. Sometimes we look worried about our mental and physical nature.

However, data is the most important resource for us because it can generate an action. This means that you need to collect and analyze data immediately to uphold a continuous flow of information. This is one of the major processes that result in the IoT revolution.

IoT Requires Artificial Intelligence

According to predictions of 2020, it is expected that there shall be many connected devices per person, data processed shall be in terabytes per second without counting in IoT. At a certain point, the internet of things shall be the largest source of data existing on the planet. And the IoT revolution can allow devices to highlight places that have opportunities.

Now, you can understand how information technologies support the transformation from old systems to advanced intelligent applications and services. To select the previous known pattern, it is important to generate a real-time data collection. But to find a method to work with this plus the data and information generated by these devices is a very big problem.

Artificial intelligence has attained a point where it can offer valuable help in speeding up tasks done by people. The moment computers can fully automate a human brain, it will result in an "intelligence explosion" that will radically change civilization. The speed of innovation shall increase exponentially. Artificial intelligence will definitely surpass the self-driving and aircraft.

AI as Part of IoT Revolution

IoT is currently creating a huge haystack of data. Many organizations are finding it difficult to make some meaning from the big amounts of data. About each large corporation is collecting and maintaining an extensive size of human-oriented data related to customers, including their purchases, preferences, and other personal information.

To conclude, the internet of things refers to data that flows between devices. To find these needles in the haystack, you must use artificial intelligence. In a few years to come, artificial intelligence can be an important element of any IoT system.

Conclusion

Artificial Intelligence and technology are one area of life that will continue to interest and surprise us with new topics, products, innovations, and new ideas. What was considered at a certain time as dumb machines have become smarter to the point where people can communicate with them on a human level. By combining with companies and other systems on their behalf, artificial intelligence makes everything that it touches smarter, and by learning as it moves on, it improves its own usability.

For companies and businesses to take advantage of AI-powered and improved interactions, the conversation has to begin inside the organization. Leaders are supposed to start with the available channels and improve their smartness. From that point, they are supposed to ask key questions about engagements with customers and employees.

The current interfaces depend on user interface design with a general limiting factor. It is significant to train the UI team to make use of AI technology and re-think interfaces without screen limitation. Much more than just another tool to assist in generating value, AI is not about how your company does things—it's who you are. In the end, we've learned AI definition, brief history, computer vision, and many more AI topics. This is not the end of AI, there is still more to learn from AI. Who knows what AI can perform to us in the future — maybe it will be a society of robots.

Mark Howard

Check Out Other Books

Go here to check out other related books that might interest you:

Kindle Fire HD 10 Manual: The Complete User Guide with Instructions, Tutorial to Unlock the True Potential of Your Kindle HD10 Fire Tablet in 30 Minutes

https://amzn.to/2zVr3rq

Alexa: How to Use Your Amazon Alexa
Devices New, Essential User Guide for Amazon
Echo and Alexa (The Complete User Guide-
Alexa & Echo Show Setup and Tips)
https://amzn.to/2NuBeFe

Kindle Fire HD 8 & 10 Tablet with Alexa: How
to Use Kindle Fire HD, the Complete User
Guide with Step-by-Step Instructions

https://amzn.to/2NMvarM

Amazon Echo Show User Guide: Amazon Echo
Show with Step-by-Step Instructions, Amazon
Echo Setup (The Complete User Guide)
https://amzn.to/2NOSdm7

Kindle Fire HD Manual: The Complete Tutorial and User Guide for Your New Kindle Fire HD Device in 30 Minutes

https://amzn.to/2AAuwMw

Fire Stick: Essential User Guide for Amazon Fire Stick, How to Unlock Your Fire Stick Like a Pro (Amazon Fire TV, Amazon Fire TV Stick, Amazon Fire TV Cube)

https://amzn.to/2Mypamo

Amazon Echo Dot - 2nd Generation Amazon Echo Dot with Alexa: How to Unlock the True Potential of Your Echo Dot, Learn to Use Your Echo Dot Like a Pro

https://amzn.to/2KZ6VVL

Kindle Fire HD8 Tablet: How to Use Kindle Fire HD, the Complete User Guide with Step-by-Step Instructions, Tutorial to Unlock the True Potential of Your Device in 30 Minutes

https://amzn.to/2Lctd6E

Alexa and Amazon Echo Dot: The Complete
User Guide with Step by Step Instructions, User
Guide to Master Your Amazon Echo Dot and
Alexa (Two Book Bundle)
https://amzn.to/2BPTpUU

Kindle Fire HD 8 & 10 Instructions: The Complete User Guide with Step by Step Instructions, Learn to Master Your Kindle Fire HD 8 & 10 Tablet in 1 Hour (Two Book Bundle)
https://amzn.to/2oi4QeK

How to Delete Books off Your Kindle: Essential Guide on How to Delete Books from Your Kindle Device and Other Useful Tips
https://amzn.to/2MJl27s

Machine Learning: An Introduction for
Beginners, User Guide to Build Intelligent
Systems

https://amzn.to/2CfGL1U

Deep Learning: Concepts and Applications for
Beginners Guide to Building Intelligent
Systems

https://amzn.to/2NPK0S0

Machine Learning and Deep Learning:
Essential User Guide to Learn and Understand
Machine Learning and Deep Learning
Effectively (Two Book Bundle)
https://amzn.to/2QzroV3

Managing Content on Your Kindle Device:
How to Deliver Content to the Kindle, Archive,
Gift, Lend, Borrow, Delete Books, Add Books,
Send and Redeem Books
https://amzn.to/2RqAgft

How to Add a Device to My Kindle Account: A
Complete Guide on How to Add Kindle Device

to My Account, How to Connect Your Digital
Devices to Your Amazon Account
https://amzn.to/2Q6DTXp

How to Use Amazon Prime Music: Everything
You Need to Know to be an Amazon Music
Pro, Tips and Tricks to Get the Most out Of
Amazon Prime Membership
https://amzn.to/2Oi1P8P